THE WASTE LAND
and
ASH WEDNESDAY

Arnold P. Hinchliffe

MACMILLAN

First published 1987

Published by
Higher and Further Education Division
MACMILLAN PUBLISHERS LTD
Houndmills, Basingstoke, Hampshire RG21 2XS
and London
Companies and representatives
throughout the world

Typeset by Wessex Typesetters
(Division of The Eastern Press Ltd)
Frome, Somerset

Printed in Hong Kong

British Library Cataloguing in Publication Data
Hinchliffe, Arnold P.
The Waste Land and Ash Wednesday.—
(The Critics debate)
1. Eliot, T.S. The Waste Land   2. Eliot, T.S.
Ash Wednesday
I. Title   II. Series
821'.912   PS3509.L43W3
ISBN 0-333-37956-X
ISBN 0-333-37957-8

• •

Contents

General Editor's Preface

OVER THE last few years the practice of literary criticism has become hotly debated. Methods developed earlier in the century and before have been attacked and the word 'crisis' has been drawn upon to describe the present condition of English Studies. That such a debate is taking place is a sign of the subject discipline's health. Some would hold that the situation necessitates a radical alternative approach which naturally implies a 'crisis situation'. Others would respond that to employ such terms is to precipitate or construct a false position. The debate continues but it is not the first. 'New Criticism' acquired its title because it attempted something fresh, calling into question certain practices of the past. Yet the practices it attacked were not entirely lost or negated by the new critics. One factor becomes clear: English Studies is a pluralistic discipline.

What are students coming to advanced work in English for the first time to make of all this debate and controversy? They are in danger of being overwhelmed by the cross-currents of critical approaches as they take up their study of literature. The purpose of this series is to help delineate various critical approaches to specific literary texts. Its authors are from a variety of critical schools and have approached their task in a flexible manner. Their aim is to help the reader come to terms with the variety of criticism and to introduce him or her to further reading on the subject and to a fuller evaluation of a particular text by illustrating the way it has been approached in a number of contexts. In the first part of the book a critical survey is given of some of the major ways the text has been appraised. This is done sometimes in a thematic manner, sometimes according to various 'schools' or 'approaches'. In the second part the authors provide their own appraisals of the text from their stated critical standpoint, allowing the reader the knowledge of their own particular approaches from which their views may in turn be evaluated. The series therein hopes to introduce and to elucidate criticism of authors and texts being studied and to encourage participation as the critics debate.

Michael Scott

Part One:
Survey

THE WASTE LAND

It has always been foolish to quarrel over The Waste
Land, *and it is self-defeating to quarrel with it.*

Grover Smith

Introduction

WHAT ELIOT actually wrote and published would fit onto a
very small shelf, but critical comment on that small shelf is
far less modest. Sheila Sullivan (1973) calls it the Eliot
industry and some of the products of that industry are very
odd. It is difficult, now, to recall the storm provoked by the
publication of *The Waste Land* or the courage displayed by his
early supporters, but from about 1930 Eliot's reputation
grows steadily until his death in 1965, when he was the
Eminent Man of Letters in the English-speaking world.
There are, Ms Sullivan detects, signs of doubt and even
disaffection and we can expect revaluation and even neglect,
but she cannot see how Eliot could be relegated from his
position as one of the two or three most influential figures in
twentieth-century literature. Much of this revaluation stems
from the gradual release of personal details. Caroline Behr
published the facts of Eliot's life and work in 1983 and Peter
Ackroyd has published an unauthorised biography (1984)
which will have to do until an authorised one appears or
even the letters (promised in 1984). But the Hayward
correspondence (Eliot took a room in John Hayward's flat in
1946 and lived there until his second marriage in 1957) and
the Emily Hale letters (some commentators suggest that
Eliot fell in love with her c. 1913) will not be released until

the twenty-first century! Such material is obviously important when discussing Eliot as 'the impersonal poet'. As far as *The Waste Land* is concerned, much information was released when Valerie Eliot published the facsimile and transcripts (including annotations by Pound) in 1971. Her introduction contained letters from Eliot not previously available, and traced the history of the poem from 1915 to the 'discovery' of the manuscript in 1968. This release of material has, however, had less effect on criticism than might have been expected.

The arrangement of so much commentary presented a problem. A chronological survey was tempting but would incur much repetition, though it would also suggest that, where early criticism stressed the impersonal, more recent criticism has focused on the personal (i.e. the biographical) elements. Robert H. Canary in his impressive study of Eliot criticism (1982) offers useful headings: 'Personal Poet', 'Impersonal Poet', 'Social Critic', 'Religious Poet', 'Traditional Poet' and 'Modern Poet' – but again there are inevitable overlaps. As far as *The Waste Land* is concerned, does the poem fit in, alongside *Ash Wednesday*, under the heading 'The Religious Poet'? According to Lyndall Gordon (1977), Eliot was a religious poet from the day he was born, but I. A. Richards (1926) put forward the view that *The Waste Land* was poetry 'severed from all beliefs'. There is much to be said for Spender's suggestion that from *The Waste Land* Eliot could have evolved in a way that justified I. A. Richards, but, as it happened, it was Christian orthodoxy which was clarified in *Four Quartets*. Eliot himself is said to have been seriously considering Buddhism, and a Buddhist is 'as immanent as a Christian in *The Waste Land*'.

Certain names are obviously important (e.g. F. R. Leavis or Cleanth Brooks) but when, exactly, did Eliot criticism begin in any serious fashion? Leonard Unger tells us that Eliot was a questionable subject for graduate research in 1938, but only ten years later he is introducing a selection of Eliot criticism where, he suggests, any approach to Eliot 'implies issues which are controversial'.

In the end I have attempted a compromise which some may call a muddle: part chronology, part headings – and I have begun at the beginning.

Storm over *The Waste Land*

Robert E. Knoll in his introduction to a collection of critical essays, *Storm over 'The Waste Land'* (1964), claims that the poem is 'the most controversial and the most influential poem of the twentieth century'. *The Waste Land* is first mentioned in 1919 but was written mainly in 1921 at Margate and Lausanne. On his return to London, Eliot showed it to Pound, who condemned its length and reduced the original 1000-line poem to its present 433 lines. Pound also advised (in 1922) against the use of 'Gerontion' as a prelude, and the manuscript was sent to John Quinn. In October 1922 the first issue of the *Criterion* published *The Waste Land*, and in November it appeared in America in the *Dial*. Its first publication in book form was on 15 December in America, and the notes were added, so Eliot said, because as a book it was too short, though Arnold Bennett recorded (10 Sep 1924) that Eliot told him the notes were serious. The first British edition was published in September 1923, by the Woolfs at the Hogarth Press. *The Waste Land* received the *Dial* award of $2000 in 1922.

As Michael Grant, editor of *T. S. Eliot: The Critical Heritage* (1982), observes, the response of early critics was both 'serious and questioning' (p. 18), though the antipathy the poem aroused was 'strong and violently felt' (p. 22). An unsigned review (26 Oct 1922)* managed to pick out two of the important strands in Eliot criticism when it described the poem as 'a collection of flashes' which were unified, since all the flashes together give 'what seems to be a complete expression of this poet's vision of modern life'. 1922 also saw Edmund Wilson's first essay on the poem, 'The Poetry of Drouth' (*Dial*, Dec),* where Wilson noted that the title, explained by a reference to Jessie Weston, was used by Eliot to suggest 'spiritual drouth' set half in the real world of contemporary London and half in medieval legend, past versus present in a complicated poem full of allusions. Too many allusions, some will say, from a poet who does not feel and who, like Prufrock, has no capacity for life, but what

* An asterisk indicates that the material is reprinted in *T. S. Eliot: The Critical Heritage*.

truth there is in that is outweighed by the feeling in the poem and its mastery of English verse. The poem 'in spite of its lack of structural unity' is one triumph after another. It is interesting to note that Wilson stresses the lack of structural unity, having already suggested a thematic unity for the poem by starting with Weston and the Grail. This question of unity is one that recurs. Gilbert Seldes (6 Dec 1922)* finds the poem at first sight 'disconnected', but a closer view reveals a hidden form dictated by the emotions in the poem. This is not a poem of ideas with an argument but rather a poem of emotions about a land that had once been fruitful but no longer is, about life that once had meaning but no longer has, themes that dictate the form of the poem. Elinor Wylie (20 Jan 1923)* also saw the poem as conceived out of 'an extremity of tragic emotion' expressed in many voices in a confused fashion, presenting weariness and despair through a stream of memories and images. But for Louis Untermeyer (17 Jan 1923)* *The Waste Land* showed only 'a pompous parade of erudition', and, while the theme (contemporary despair, breaking-down) might dictate the form, an artist, surely, is pledged to give form to the formless? Such a poem might have *documentary* value – the world has suffered a loss of values – but it signally fails to recognise that the world is also groping for new ones. This is a view echoed by Harriet Monroe (Mar 1923),* who notes that, if Eliot's poem gives us 'the malaise of our time', there is a whole world outside which the poem does not recognise. Men of science, inventors and engineers are creating a modern world against which poets in London and Montmartre merely inveigh gloomily.

Conrad Aiken, in *An Anatomy of Melancholy,** attacked both the use of allusions and the plan (or lack of it). The allusions may have value for Eliot, but can they have any value for us even with the footnotes? Aiken suggests that allusions to the Fisher King or the Grail legend even when explained do not make themselves felt. Aiken also objected to Eliot's plan – 'oddly akin to planlessness' – and rejected the idea fostered by admiring critics that what we have here is a 'kind of epic in a walnut shell'. The poem's value is emotional and the separate poems must be taken (as they are offered) as 'a series of sharp, discrete, slightly related perceptions and feelings, dramatically and lyrically present and violently

juxtaposed', to give us the impression of a modern
consciousness that sees itself in fragments. On a plot level
any bit could be dropped without serious damage to the
poem (and he suggests several episodes), but this would ruin
the 'emotional ensemble'. The poem, in short, succeeds as a
'powerful, melancholy tone-poem' and the notes only give it
a 'sour air of pedantry'.

Charles Powell in the *Manchester Guardian* (31 Oct 1923)*
and F. L. Lucas (3 Nov 1923)* were but two critics who
objected to pedantry and parody, while Gorham B. Munson,
in a very long essay (1 July 1924),* tackled the esoteric
nature of a poem which, he suggested, summed up Eliot's
intellectual and emotional attitudes. The esoteric nature of
the poem he describes as deliberate mystification, but he saw
that the unity of the poem depended upon Eliot's personality
presenting a state of mind reflected in broken forms. But, he
pointed out, there has already been a great deal of poetry of
melancholy and drouth, so writing about this mood should
not have been difficult. Yet to understand the poem the
reader has eleven pages of notes, needs a few foreign
languages and much diligence to track down the allusions,
only to find that he has discovered something 'quite ordinary'.
The Waste Land is not for the general reader but for a chosen
coterie of like-minded people who will see in it the modern
cultural situation and the European mind. But the American
mind has boundless energy and America has hope where
Europe can only find hopelessness and resignation. When
America realises its responsibility in the present crisis it will
respond with daring and curiosity.

Contemporary reaction, then, either saw the poem as true
and a masterpiece or, in Amy Lowell's view, a piece of tripe.
All the problems the poem throws up were immediately
recognised. Is the poem social or personal? Has the poem
unity or is it in fragments which may then be justified as
unity by its themes? Are the allusions resonant or just erudite
gibberish? And, lastly, is the poem un-American in ignoring
modern science and the future and hankering after the past?
For in leaving America Eliot was turning his back on
optimism as well as his roots. William Carlos Williams
(*Harvard Advocate*, 125, Dec 1938) felt that there had been a
deterioration in Eliot's work since he left America, while Van

Wyck Brooks (1952) notes that it was in the faith that men had the capacity to govern themselves that America came into existence, and that the main body of the American tradition, as literature expressed it, showed this faith until the beginning of the First World War. It was the tradition of Jefferson that men could dispense with authority and be trusted with freedom, and Brooks comments that the only strand of tradition that Eliot ignored was the tradition of the country in which he had grown up. Indeed, he seems not merely to ignore it but to be actively hostile to it.

Whether *The Waste Land* was unpatriotic or not remains, probably, the last question to be asked of the poem. Frank Kermode's essay 'Reading Eliot Today' (1963)* suggests that it was after all a rather genteel storm, but he reminds us that 'Modern Poetry' still connotes Eliot, and *The Waste Land* is still, after forty years, a modern poem if only because the term 'modern' has partly turned into a period concept, like 'Baroque'. But we no longer see Eliot as related to the past in the way he proposes. Now Eliot is part of the romantic tradition he excoriated, and the technical devices are now matters 'for cool historical explanation'. *The Waste Land* remains a difficult poem and it must have bewildered its first readers, yet for many there was the belief that fuller understanding would come and a sense of unity below the explanations.

Milestones

Some voices spoke with authority. In 1926 I. A. Richards added an appendix entitled 'The Poetry of T. S. Eliot' to his *Principles of Literary Criticism*, noting that *The Waste Land* had produced much bewilderment ('irritated or enthusiastic'), which had many sources, but the most important was the absence of any 'coherent intellectual thread' on which items of the poem could be strung. Richards felt that the search for such a thread was pointless, since the unity of the poem was in the 'accord, contrast, and interaction of their emotional effects' and not in any intellectual scheme. A second source of worry was the use of allusions which many readers thought were a cause to admire the author's wit or, worse, his erudition, when in fact they were there for the sake of the 'emotional aura which they bring and the attitudes they incite'. Allusion was a device for compression and without it *The Waste Land* would need twelve books, since in content it is the equivalent of an epic. A third objection is that the poem is obscure and/or ambiguous, but great works are necessarily both in their immediate effect (the same, Richards suggests, could be said of *Hamlet!*). The real question is whether the hard work needed to resolve the poem is worthwhile. A reader must cope with Jessie Weston and Dante and evaluate the central position of Tiresias, but we must not try to catch the poem in an intellectual net or squeeze doctrine out of it. Eliot's poetry can be summed up as 'the music of ideas' and, if the poem contains all kinds of ideas, they are there to be responded to, not worked out. Only people who cannot read poetry could resist Eliot's rhythms, which bring alive every fragment.

This brief survey seemed to have got most things right and it lent weight to all subsequent accounts of Eliot's work. In 1931 Edmund Wilson published *Axel's Castle*, which looked at literature between 1870 and 1930 and took as its theme the idea that the literary history of our time was the development of Symbolism and its fusion or conflict with Naturalism. In the chapter on T. S. Eliot, Wilson suggested that the present was more timid than the past. The bourgeois were afraid to let themselves go – a theme looked at by French writers but now tackled by Eliot, though from a somewhat different, American point of view. The principal subject of Eliot's work is 'regret at situations unexplored, that dark rankling of passions inhibited' which we find in American writers from Hawthorne to Henry James and Edith Wharton, and the most complete expression of this theme of emotional starvation is to be found in *The Waste Land*, where, according to Wilson, we can quickly identify the sterility as the sterility of the Puritan temperament. The colonisation of New England by Puritans was merely incidental in the rise of the middle-class, which brought commercial–industrial civilisation to European cities and American ones. *The Waste Land* looks at the dreariness of great modern cities, places of desolation but also anarchy and doubt. In the post-war world of shattered institutions, strained nerves and bankrupt ideals, life no longer seems 'serious or coherent'.

A year later, in 1932, F. R. Leavis published *New Bearings in English Poetry: A Study of the Contemporary Situation*, which was reprinted in 1950 with a 'Retrospect'. In this added material Leavis sees his study as about a particular time and by now itself a historical fact and one which altered the view of poetry. Already by 1935, when Matthiessen published his book on Eliot, there had been a change of attitude, and Matthiessen can complain that Leavis seemed to be writing 'continually on the defensive' as if he were single-handedly trying to convert an unappreciative world. But Leavis recalls the difficulties facing him in putting forward a serious treatment of Eliot. Leavis's position at Cambridge was always difficult, but his criticism, as George Steiner points out (1967, p. 254), was rooted in a changing sensibility and his achievement was to give that change 'its most precise and cogent critical justification'. After Eliot and Pound it was becoming difficult to maintain that Tennyson and Swinburne were major forces directing English poetry. Leavis began from the assumption that poetry matters little to the modern world. Victorian poetry inherited its values from the Romantic poets, but, where those poets had been able to believe that their poetry could move the world, the Victorian poets saw the world as alien, unpoetical, and no protest was worth making 'except for the protest of withdrawal'. The problem for a modern poet, therefore, was to invent a technique that could reflect ways of feeling or modes of experience for adult moderns, and Eliot's importance was that he had made a start.

Leavis was enthusiastic about both the allusions and the 'rich disorganization' of the poem, pointing out that the former allows Eliot to present the state of civilisation with a compression he could not otherwise achieve. Anthropology serves to contrast the remoteness of our civilisation from natural rhythms and functions positively in evoking that 'particular sense of the unity of life which is essential to the poem'. Tiresias is seen as the attempt to impose or focus on 'an inclusive human consciousness', while the organisation of the poem may be called, by analogy, musical. If this is a poem for a limited public with special knowledge, most of the special knowledge would be available to the public who would read modern poetry. The poem is difficult ('and a full response comes only with familiarity'), but its general method and nature should be obvious at first reading, and Leavis analyses 'The Burial of the Dead' to show how it works and demonstrate 'obvious themes and transitions' (1932, p. 91ff.). The way in which Eliot manages the transitions within the parts of the poem and between them is a positive achievement and a new start for English poetry.

For F. O. Matthiessen, however, Eliot's achievements were firmly located in his American background. *The Achievement of T. S. Eliot: An Essay on the Nature of Poetry* was published in 1935 (revised in 1947) and Matthiessen's approach is made clear in the Preface (and the subtitle of his book): he intends to consider the methods and achievements of Eliot and discuss the fundamental nature of poetry now obscured by a tendency to treat it 'as a social document' (p. vii). He sees Eliot in reaction to the individualism of the America into which he was born. His desire to link himself with a tradition comes from his revulsion 'against the lawless exploitation by which late nineteenth-century American individuals made any coherent society impossible' (p. 144). Eliot had to meet the problem of the contemporary artist who possesses knowledge of the past, of all pasts, to a degree hardly possible a century ago. It is this realisation of everything happening at once that can lead to chaos or, if the artist can find the pattern, unity. Eliot's pattern was anthropology, myth and Jessie Weston. Matthiessen insists that the reader is enchanted by the movement of the lines in the poem and then the mind furnishes information as with, say, Milton. When reading Milton, a modern reader has to remind himself of certain details which were once common property among educated readers but are now increasingly forgotten. The reader of a contemporary poem has to get used to a procedure that is unfamiliar and that does not meet our preconceptions of what poetry ought to be. Thus in his chapter entitled 'The Auditory Imagination' Matthiessen examines Eliot's feeling for rhythms in poetry that are 'far below conscious levels of thought' and refers us to the essay on Dante with its statement that poetry communicates before it is understood.

The structure (discussed by Matthiessen in chapter 3) is seen as self-contained and based on an externalised structure of parallel myths given further focus by sifting the material through the eye of a central observer, Tiresias, whose power to foresuffer all can embrace the contrasts and likenesses packed into a short poem – the luxury of the upper class, the uninspired bourgeois existence and the poor talking in a pub (p. 60). Matthiessen also pointed to the large number of styles in the poem and, indeed, in Eliot's work as a whole, though this should not blind us to what Matthiessen (locating unity once more in feeling and tone) called 'the tenacity of Eliot's preoccupations' (p. 101).

Four years later, in 1939, Cleanth Brooks published his *Modern Poetry and the Tradition*, which looks at *The Waste Land* in chapter 7. This chapter is often referred to as the grandfather of all *explications de texte* and looks forward to Williamson (1953), Southam (1969) and particularly Grover Smith (1956). Like Brooks, Williamson, for example, sees the anthropological framework as a means rather than an end, but, where, for Brooks, fertility myths hold the promise of resurrection, for Williamson they also involve the poem in the mysteries of sexuality, allowing Williamson to keep personal levels of significance in the poem. But, where Brooks can see the Fisher King, at the end of the poem, as prepared for fruitful action (which will take place in *Ash Wednesday*), Williamson finds him 'knowing but helpless'. Brooks is, of course, endowing the poem with strong Christian values. His method of 'explaining' the poem also suggests the method followed by many critics: namely, the judicious selection of certain images or symbols by which the poem becomes a unity and meaningful. Brooks insists that a knowledge of the symbols taken from Jessie Weston is essential for an understanding of the poem, and that its basic method is contrast: the contrast between two kinds of life and two kinds of death. He refers us to Eliot's essay on Baudelaire (1921), where the loss of the knowledge of good and evil means that the inhabitants of the Waste Land are not alive. His analysis of the poem section by section challenges the view that this is a statement of despair and disillusionment (poetry of drouth) and seeks to prove that the poem is a unified whole and does not work through simply irony or simple contrast. There is, Brooks suggests, a gradual reinforcing of symbols which leads the poem finally to become a poem of belief. He argues that the Christian terminology in the poem is, for the poet, a mass of clichés which must be brought alive again. To do this requires a radical method, since Eliot aims to revitalise symbols that have been 'crusted over with distorting familiarity'. The reader, therefore, must register surface similarities which, through irony, are revealed as dissimilar, as later this association of dissimilarities is itself revealed to be superficial – 'the chains of likeness are in reality fundamental'. Thus for Brooks the statement of belief emerges '*through* confusion and cynicism – not in spite of them'.

The most radical (but simple) treatment of this tangle is probably that offered by Charles Moorman (1960), who solves the problem of unity with the following formula: unity = myth, therefore the poem must be religious (and about sex, too!). Talk of fertility rites is pertinent, but the myth at the heart is religious; therefore the poem must be religious. It is a commonplace that the interpretation of *The Waste Land* lies in analysing the use of myth in the poem, and critics have frequently complained that this is merely to impose a mechanical unity on the poem: Eliot puts a scene from myth or literature close to a scene from modern life, and then leaves us to work out the effect of the comparison. But, apart from this mechanical unity, there must also be organic unity. Critics have objected that the poem contains 'too great a variety of comparisons to have any one organically unifying principle' (Moorman 1960, p. 134), and Moorman concedes that at first glance the poem is a hodgepodge. But in fact all the images and the comparisons boil down to one image and one comparison: the basic metaphor involves the waste land of Arthurian myth. The influence of Jessie Weston is important, and her interpretation of that myth is primarily sexual – castration, wounded virility which blights the land and the cup and lance, which, in the Christian story, become the Grail and the Bleeding Lance. Weston's version of the myth is the objective correlative for Eliot's own emotions about modern society and his life in it: the modern world is a waste land devastated 'by moral and spiritual wounds that have affected its reproductive organs and creative functions', giving a central image of sexual sterility as a foundation for all the metaphorical allusions in the poem. Many commentators (and Moorman cites Grover Smith) have interpreted the allusions as sexual and Christian: *The Waste*

Land 'summarizes the Grail legend', as Grover Smith puts it. This allows not merely unity but also the presence of a sacramental point of view, which Moorman illustrates, concluding that this kind of unity is far from mechanical. Tiresias, he suggests, not only sees but feels too; he is not compared to but identified with the modern lovers. The difficulty is that the reader – 'perhaps unfairly' – is expected to bring in the full weight of situations that are merely alluded to. For Eliot the Arthurian myth was the perfect objective correlative to express his own disillusion and disgust; moreover, it involved not merely fertility versus sterility but 'more particularly religious fertility and secular sterility'. In later versions the only cure was in the resanctification of the Fisher King and his rededication to his mission. The only cure for the waste land (and, in Eliot's eyes, the modern world) is religious in nature.

These critics are all writing, of course, after Eliot's conversion (1927) and the publication of *Dante* (1929) and *Ash Wednesday* (1930), but a persistent idea of belief in the poem begins to shift it from social document to personal confession.

The impersonal poet?

In fact, critics had always detected personal feeling in the poem, and in 'Thoughts after Lambeth' (1931) Eliot rejected the idea of *The Waste Land* as a piece of social criticism, claiming that it was only 'a personal and wholly insignificant grouse against life', 'a piece of rhythmical grumbling'. Randall Jarrell's description of Eliot (quoted Bush 1984) as 'one of the most subjective and daemonic poets who ever lived, the victim and helpless beneficiary of his own inexorable compulsions [and] obsessions' seems true, though it hardly fits in with Hugh Kenner's 'Invisible Poet' (1959). But as early as 1925 Eliot ordered that there should be no biography, and a memorandum attached to his will requested that there be none – a request his widow and Faber and Faber are trying to observe though under such circumstances speculation creeps in. The letters are promised (edited by Mrs Eliot) and some early material has been released (*Poems Written in Early*

Youth, 1967); we have too, of course, Mrs Eliot's facsimile edition of *The Waste Land*. Criticism has, of late, tended to stress the personal where early criticism stressed the impersonal, though early critics were naturally responding to Eliot's statement in 'Tradition and the Individual Talent' (1919) that poetry is 'not the expression of personality, but an escape from personality'. Even then, with typical Eliotic carefulness, the poet reminds his readers that only those who have a personality and emotions can know what it means to escape from them. Hugh Kenner also points out that invisibility was practical sense. Here was a fairly anonymous foreigner, about thirty years old, who was doing reviews, articles or what he could, and who capitalised on his anonymity by playing a role: the role that suited the magazine for which he was writing and that gave Eliot 'the freedom of a whimsical but purposeful *Poltergeist*' (1959, p. 83). The personae he invented for this work appear in the poems, too, where Kenner thinks of them as pseudo-persons. Prufrock, for example, is a name plus a voice but not a character (is he young or old or just middle-aged?). Hence we have the generic Eliot 'character' – Gerontion is another of his metamorphoses – of which the extreme case is Tiresias, who may be the most important personage in *The Waste Land* but who remains a spectator: what he sees is the substance of the poem and he is what he sees. Kenner looks at the influence of Bradley (Eliot's Harvard dissertation *Knowledge and Experience in the Philosophy of F. H. Bradley* appeared in 1916), who is mentioned in the notes. According to Kenner, reading Bradley assisted Eliot in three ways: it provided him with a point of view towards history (hence the essay 'Tradition and the Individual Talent'); it liberated him from the Laforgue-inspired posture of an ironist by affirming that all personality was artificial, including the one we suppose to be our own; and it acquitted him of eccentricity because he avoided (for personal reasons) a more normal way of presenting material. And, since Bradley arrives at no conclusions and certainly no incitement to action, the poem could be a loose medley. But Eliot, preoccupied with drama and particularly seventeenth-century drama, saw a long poem as somebody's monologue – both Prufrock and Gerontion present us with a view of society and civilisation, but also a perceiving – indeed, a presiding – consciousness. So Eliot produced a note on *The Waste Land* to give that poem a point of view which had at least a name. Kenner's analysis of the poem concludes that it is full of 'functional obscurity', but its success was precisely that it expressed for many readers their sense of 'not knowing what to do with themselves' or, as Eliot later put it, the illusion of being disillusioned.

Much of what Kenner writes suggests that he was aware that 'invisible' might well mean 'hidden', and for personal reasons. For C. K. Stead (1964), Eliot's problem with form was aesthetic. At the end of the nineteenth century Romanticism was split between popular poets with an audience and the Aesthetes in search of Beauty (which only an artist could perceive), and Eliot (with his undivided sensibility) wanted to correct the relationship with the audience, avoiding the contemporary prescription, write what the audience wants and prettily *or* ignore the audience. Eliot, like a chameleon, adapted as audiences changed. In early essays he seemed to take the aesthetic attitude, but, once there was an audience willing to read modern poetry on its own terms, then the aesthetic attitude began to relax. Stead points to three essays: 'Tradition and the Individual Talent', 'Jonson' and '*Hamlet*', all apparently about tradition and showing Eliot at the time preoccupied with the process of poetry in which the conscious will plays the minor role of sub-editor. Stead's comments suggest a kind of composition as dependent on imagination or inspiration as any Romantic poet could have wished. The escape from personality is an escape from opinion and rhetoric which had marred poetry in the mid-nineteenth century – 'not away from self, but deeper into the self, "below the levels of consciousness"' (p. 131). Thus, although critics have seen *The Waste Land* as a discourse with the links in the chain suppressed, it is a self-contained poetical entity that works if it 'modifies and enriches the sensibility of the reader' (p. 148). In a poem by Keats, Tennyson or Milton we see (whatever else is in the poem) 'a sequence, a temporal (narrative), or spatial (descriptive), or logical structure', but *The Waste Land* aspires to the quality of music. The first impression is not, as critics would have us believe, deceptive: the only unifying principle is that all the states of feeling have their common origin in the mind of one man. Thus, if we look back at a poem such as 'Prufrock', we discover that it was put together from a number of sections rather like *The Waste Land*. Some of the lines were written at Harvard, some in Paris and some in Germany, but it does not suffer, because its coherence depends on consistency of feeling rather than a sequence of ideas or events. Stead, therefore, looks with approval on those critics who saw that *The Waste Land* was held together by feeling: to I. A. Richards, who found its unity in 'emotional effects' rather than 'an intellectual scheme that analysis must work out'; to R. P. Blackmur, who saw *The Waste Land* as neither an allegory nor metaphysics in verse, but as poetry; and, of course, to Leavis, who found unity in an inclusive consciousness, and an organisation that was musical and exhibited no progression. But, as more and more material about the poem has appeared, the fact that Eliot 'went to the trouble of transmuting this material into non-discursive form is ignored' (Stead 1964, p. 162). Thus we are given a poem-by-poem analysis by George Williamson which suggests 'the basic scheme' for a poem such as *The Waste Land*. Looking at one passage ('The Fire Sermon') and the explication of it by Brooks, D. E. S. Maxwell and Williamson, Stead notes that each critic looks for details which are *significant*, and 'significance' means the 'ease with which the chosen details can be accommodated in an abstract system of ideas' (p. 164). What Stead would like is an illiterate audience (as in 'The Use of Poetry', where Eliot claimed that, since poetry is primarily an aural emotional experience, like listening to music, the intellect can easily impede the full and unified experience of poetry). Stead would not deny all validity to a discussion of anthropology and symbolism, but feels that there is a strong danger that these will substitute for the poem. Again this sounds plausible, but the musical analogy hides the problem of what – whether illiterate or not – we are responding to. Feeling, but what kind of feeling? How far, for example, is it religious feeling as noted by Leavis and Brooks?

According to Lyndall Gordon (1977), Eliot wrote his biography poem by poem, and they show the character of a man who sees his life as 'a religious quest despite the anti-religious mood of his age and the distracting claims of women, friends and alternative careers' (p. 1); who was on the edge of conversion in 1914 but who, having failed to come alive through religion, decided to fall in love, saying that passion, sexual passion, may mean 'the only possible escape from a prosaic world' (p. 72). But marriage turned out to mean, after a brief period of liberation, only grim responsibility. In the poetry Eliot moved, Gordon points out, from 'St Narcissus' to 'Gerontion', from a failed religious character to a post-war contemporary character who deplores the lack of commitment and the unenlightened death he faces, while in writing about the pilgrim of *The Waste Land* Eliot invokes exemplary lives (Dante, Christ, Augustine, Ezekiel, the Grail Knight), who always had a dark period before conversion and/or initiation. Looking at the manuscript drafts for the poems, Gordon concludes that Pound's editing served to blot out the autobiography and allow the cultural statement to dominate the poem. Not unreasonably the critics fastened on the cultural aspects of the poem as it was presented to them, but Eliot, writing to Richard Aldington in 1922, said that the poem for him was now a thing of the past, that critics saw despair and erudition rather than recognising them as facets of an exemplary life. For Gordon, the poem started as a personal record of a man who saw himself as a candidate for the religious life but was impeded by his nature and distracted by domestic claims. He was writing a spiritual autobiography in an age uncongenial to that sort of writing and so sought to get at his audience by indirection (a method he was later to employ in his comedies). But his strategy (presenting himself as a child of the times) was too successful, and readers ignored the would-be saint. So here, too, we return to the alternatives of sainthood and marriage fruitfully contained in fertility myths.

The facts about this marriage leave much to guesswork. A girl called Vivienne is mentioned in a letter on 26 April 1915, and on 26 June Eliot married Vivienne Haigh-Wood. Eliot's father died in January 1919, and that year *The Waste Land* is also mentioned. Eliot's mother visited Eliot in 1921; that year *The Waste Land* was partly on paper (letter to Quinn, 9 May), and in October Eliot went to Margate and in November to Lausanne, where most of the original version (about 1000 lines) was written. Eliot returned to London in mid-December to show the poem to Pound, who reduced it to its final length. The breakdown during which the poem was written is generally ascribed to three factors: an unhappy marriage, the death of Eliot's father and the visit of his mother, each and all of which have inspired biographical and psychological explanations. The unhappy marriage is often cited as the source of much of Eliot's early work, and some details can be found in, for instance, volume II of Bertrand Russell's *Autobiography*, covering the period 1914–44. Russell taught Eliot at Harvard (and can claim to have given Eliot the vision of London as an unreal city which figures in the opening part of the poem). In a letter (July 1915) Russell describes Vivienne as 'light, a little vulgar, adventurous, full of life', but unable to stimulate Eliot, who was ashamed of his marriage. Russell insists that he did not find Eliot's wife attractive and had no sexual relations with her. William Empson (1972), reviewing the facsimile of *The Waste Land*, pointed out that Eliot seemed to have piled up sketches in the hope of finding a theme for them, and so was hardly surprised when Pound threw half of them out. But what was the theme that Pound thought he recognised and admired? Empson believes that it was something we now find incidental: London had just escaped the First World War and was to be destroyed in the next because it was in the hands of international financiers – a theme dear to Pound's heart. But the edition is keen to insist on the private theme of the poem, which one would expect to be about the first wife, ill and perhaps already starting to go mad. The edition, however, specifically rejects that. Just before writing *The Waste Land*, Eliot was so ill that his wife arranged for him to see a specialist, and he took three months sick-leave from the bank. Vivienne went with him to Margate because Eliot, who was supposed to be alone, could not bear the idea of being alone. Both Eliot and Vivienne had nervous illnesses, and these seem to have drawn them together. Vivienne much admired 'A Game of Chess' and makes, from the edition, a good impression. For Empson the facts suggest that the marriage did not really go wrong until at least five years later, so the grouse must be something quite different. In 1919 Eliot wrote to Quinn that he needed to bring out some kind of book in America before he visited his family. His parents felt that he had made a mess of his life living abroad, and making a disastrous marriage and a book might appease them. His father died and his will made it clear that any inheritance was in trust, reverting to the family on his son's death, thus depriving Vivienne of any benefits should Eliot die. The mother's visit was clearly a disappointment, and Empson suggests that this 'terrifyingly energetic' seventy-seven year old refused to sleep under the same roof as Eliot's wife or to budge in the matter of his father's will. So for Empson the real central symbol is a father (hence echoes from *The Tempest* and the essay on *Hamlet*, which was written in September 1919).

Either the unhappy marriage or a terrifying mother might explain the women in Eliot's poetry. If one looks at Herbert Howarth (1965), Vivienne does not appear in the index (nor does any mention of the marriage), giving some substance to critics such as Arthur Sampley (1968), who suggests that an unhappy first marriage explains the absence of attractive women in Eliot's work, a topic explored by Tony Pinkney (1984). Pinkney's subject is the role and tribulations of women in Eliot's poetry, and his method rests upon the research of Melanie Klein and D. W. Winnicott. But Pinkney insists that his reading is guided throughout by a maxim from Eliot's own creation, Sweeney, who claims that

> Any man has to, needs to, wants to
> Once in a lifetime, do a girl in.

That the women in Eliot's poetry trouble many readers – they seem to be uniformly disagreeable, neurotic or mad and, what is worse, presented with disgust and/or contempt – is true, but whether this approach is helpful remains doubtful. The unpleasantness (in tone and content) of the portrayal of women has given rise to some wild speculations, of which more later. Pinkney's guides, Klein and Winnicott, apparently delve behind the Oedipus complex into the most primitive phases of the relationship between an infant and its mother, and their insights have a claim on feminist criticism, focusing attention on the representations of the mother and the female body – here applied to Eliot. The language used by Pinkney is frankly uncongenial to paraphrase and the author himself cheerfully concedes at the end that poetry resists being shrunk to the dimensions of a case study. *The Waste Land* was drafted during convalescence from some kind of breakdown caused by overwork, financial worries and tensions from a bad marriage and with the family in America. Hence Pinkney suggests we should give some weight to the Conrad epigraph, which Eliot found appropriate and 'somewhat elucidative'. Pinkney argues that this epigraph stressed the subjective origins of the text, stripping it of any pretension to being 'an impersonal survey of cultural decay': the journey up the Congo in *Heart of Darkness*, like Eliot climbing a staircase, was, Pinkney suggests, 'a penetration into the maternal body'. The epigraph we now have is from Petronius (where a male audience is marshalled against a female victim), which looks back to the *Satyricon*, itself the founding text in the genre (or anti-genre) of the *menippea*, a genre which flouts the idea of organic unity and narrative point of view and which is busily unravelled 'into an unresolvable plurality of conflicting voices'. This 'form' is immediately challenged by Tiresias, who unites all the rest in his person and leaves us with a poem that is a dramatic monologue governed by a single consciousness and which will therefore sustain a narrative as shapely as a Victorian novel. With the publication of drafts and the facsimile, however, a further problem emerges, since we can now see Pound's hand at work; and what may be needed at some time is a study that would consider *The Waste Land* as a Poundian psychoanalytical text in its own right (Pinkney 1984, p. 98)! By reinstating passages that were deleted, the interpreter, Pinkney admits, can have his/her own way, and he chooses the fishing-expedition deleted from 'Death by Water'. He does remind us, however, that the original Tiresias was successively male and female (and then male), but Eliot makes him explicitly hermaphrodite, which allows him to unite two figures: the drowned Ophelia and the drowned Phlebas. This in turn leads (though a complicated scenario) to Agamemnon and Clytemnestra and the avenging Orestes 'violently disposed to wrest the phallus away from the mother' (p. 101). Thus the absent centre of *The Waste Land* which the poem (and the poet?) cannot fully acknowledge is 'precisely an Orestian phantasy of attack on the mother'.

In his preface Pinkney attributes the origin of his book to a woman who persuaded him to lock away his Leavis, but one wonders if that was entirely wise. There had been earlier psychological interpretations that were less sexist. Thus Harry Trosman (1974) furnishes information on Roger Vittox, the Swiss psychologist who treated Eliot when the poem was being written and also considers Eliot's alienation from his father and the need for maternal support (a triangle, it is claimed, also reflected in the Russell, Vivienne and Eliot relationship). Psychologists have always been tempted to see Eliot's work as full of Oedipal imagery and fears of castration. Elizabeth Drew (1949) offered a Jungian interpretation. Stimulated by an article by Genevieve W. Foster (1945), she finds a parallel between Jung's description of dream symbols arising during what he called 'the integration of personality' and the images used in Eliot's poetry during his development, and, though she concedes that psychology has its limitations and makes a poor critical instrument, Eliot's poetry shows, she believes, a parallel development of materials cited by Jung and confirms his belief in certain archetypal patterns which recur and are of great significance. Tradition is the inherited wisdom of the race, and Jung saw the collective unconscious as 'the unconscious inherited wisdom of the race', which helps us to account for recurring imagery in dreams – primordial images or archetypes – which appear when an individual is brought by particular circumstances into touch with some aspect of collective universal experience modified by personal circumstances and the personal temperament of the dreamer, but always suggesting involvement in larger, more impersonal forces. Thus Drew relates Jung's archetype of transformation to aspects of *The Waste Land* while reminding us that we need not accept the theory, since Eliot knew the sources of his symbols and used them with the *conscious* manipulation of an artist. Drew's treatment of the actual poem is sensitive in a conventional way, but the supposed Jungian insights seem to be recalled only in occasional footnotes. Perhaps it would be sensible to suggest that, whatever biographical facts we have that are capable of psychoanalytical study, we should distinguish between the sources, personal and/or literary (and the two may be the same), and what comes out of the poet's struggle with his material. Certainly speculation can lead anywhere.

The dedication of the early poems to Jean Verdenal, for example, led to suggestions of an attachment and so to the homosexual interpretation of *The Waste Land*. T. S. Matthews (1974) is probably right when he suggests that not much can be made of the friendship between Eliot and Verdenal, and that there may have been some exaggeration in Eliot's 'melancholy remembrance of this foreign friend'. It was John Peter (1952) who offered the first statement of this idea, and the essay caused such offence that Eliot, through his lawyers, suppressed it. Virtually unprocurable for seventeen years, it was finally reprinted in 1969 with a postscript. At this distance it is difficult to see what the fuss was about. Peter points out that, if *The Waste Land* is the most discussed poem of our age, discussion has done little to make it more intelligible to an unsophisticated audience. What is needed is some single thread to guide the reader to the point where he could pass on to critics such as Leavis, Matthiessen and Brooks. Until 'some simpler and more palpable epitome' of the poem's meaning is found, the result will only be perplexity and confusion. Taking, therefore, the line that the poem is variations on a theme (with the theme omitted), Peter offers as that theme a stage direction ('rather clumsy', he admits) about the situation of the protagonist of the poem, a man who at some previous time has fallen in love with a young man who met his death by drowning. (An appropriate parallel, Peter suggests, would be Tennyson's *In Memoriam*.) Enough time has now passed since this death for the speaker to realise that his love is irreplaceable, and the monologue of the poem is effectively a meditation on this, upon his horrified reactions to it and of the bleak world which remains without his love. This young man, Peter tentatively suggests (in the postscript), might have been Jean Verdenal, to whom the Prufrock volume was dedicated and who is recalled as waving a branch of lilac (and was drowned in the mud of Gallipoli). George Watson (1976) was able, in fact, to find out very little about Verdenal (except that he was neither tall nor particularly handsome, and that he did not drown at sea) and finds the homoerotic interpretation both 'unproven' and 'trivial', but Peter's article stimulated (or overstimulated) James E. Miller (1977), who offered 'a radically new reading of *The Waste Land*'.

Miller points out that Brooks and the New Criticism stressed the divorce between biography and literature, that poetry was not emotion nor was it an idea, a statement that might be paraphrased; and so gradually developed a general interpretation of the poem as a pessimistic view of the modern world, asserting that modern man lived a futile life in a world where all faith and belief had been reduced to enigmatic fragments (p. 8). But Eliot himself and the publication of the facsimile suggested the personal nature of the poem. Thus Eliot's praise for *In Memoriam* and how he read that poem is a pattern for us in reading *The Waste Land*. But, having warned us of 'reductive interpretations', in much of what follows Miller argues in a circle. It was, we are told, the death of Verdenal which propelled Eliot into a hasty marriage. That Eliot's marriage was doomed to breakdown is certain, but Empson is probably correct in suggesting it was not breaking down during the composition of *The Waste Land*, and Miller's blunt assertion that Eliot handed over his wife to 'the well-known satyr Bertrand Russell' (p. 24) needs qualifying; many would agree with Spender's assessment of Russell's role as generous, practical and rational. The role of Eliot's father is dismissed, leaving the marriage central, but Miller at least provides interpretations of poems that have had little critical attention – 'The Death of St Narcissus' and the 'Ode', which was suppressed, a fact that Miller finds significant. The 'Ode' is interpreted as recording Eliot's loss of poetic inspiration, his disastrous honeymoon and regret over Verdenal, but, though the poem is remarkably difficult (E. P. Bollier concluded that the incoherence of the last strophe was quite genuine), the presence of Verdenal seems gratuitous. For Miller *The Waste Land* was written as a very personal poem responding to pressures and feelings that Eliot himself did not fully understand. But Pound disturbed the structure, so Eliot added the notes and the idea of Tiresias as a central consciousness imposed on what was left of the poem.

Miller tests his theory with detailed analysis which is not entirely persuasive; thus the two scenes in 'A Game of Chess' are not a commentary on modern marriage but express a personal revulsion, brought on by 'emotional paralysis caused by the death of his friend whose memory haunts him', against sexuality in marriage, while in part v it is Vivienne Eliot who asks whether the third party to their marriage is a man or a woman. Weston's book appeared in 1920, when Eliot was going through a critical time, and Miller's summary is, to say the least, creative: 'We might assume' that he found the book, and detected parallels between himself and the Fisher-King; the most striking parallel 'perhaps' would be impotence, but this would have been preceded by a deep wound (the loss of Verdenal) which caused his impotence, though ('of course') psychoanalysis would 'no doubt' trace that impotence to childhood. It was impotence that caused him to see a waste land all about him, to convert London to Dante's Hell and to see sexual depravity everywhere he looked (p. 94). Yet Miller objects to Kermode's description of this kind of reading as the 'homosexual interpretation' (*Atlantic Monthly*, 1972) and tells us finally that what happened between Verdenal and Eliot is not our concern, which lies rather with what he did with it in his poetry! Verdenal seems not to provide a particularly useful guide through *The Waste Land*.

Cross-currents

There are, obviously, problems about *The Waste Land* and objections more serious than simple dislike or incomprehension. Karl Shapiro (1960), for example, is splendidly intemperate when writing about Eliot. He suggests that the poem is completely lacking in unity and that what keeps it going is rhetoric. The switches from description to exclamation to expletive are, it is true, managed beautifully, but the proof of its failure (which some will think an odd sort of proof) is that no one, not even Eliot, has been able to proceed from it, and its influence lies entirely outside literature.

The disconnectedness disturbs Graham Hough (1960), too, but his response is more urgent and serious. Hough looks at Eliot's translation of and introduction to St-John Perse's *Anabasis* (1930), where, perhaps, we can see Eliot discovering unity in his own poem as he had found it in his essay on Joyce and the mythic method. What, according to Eliot, marks out St-John Perse is *tone*. Though, throughout the poem, the voice may vary in pitch inflexions, it is, fundamentally, constant, and while we enjoy the richness of effects we can still recognise that it is the same voice. Through this voice the character of the hero emerges, and through this character the obscurities of the poem disappear. The symbols in *Anabasis* derive their magnificence from the fact that they embody 'an unbelievable number of recollections and evocations', and the poem is obscure because links in the chain of meaning have been suppressed. The reader has to learn to allow the images to fall into the mind without asking why until, at the end, 'a total effect is produced'. The selection of images is neither chaotic nor perverse because, Eliot insists, there is a logic of the imagination which people unable to read poetry cannot understand. And even those who can understand should not depend on first impressions, since it was not until Eliot had read the poem five or six times that he was persuaded of Perse's success. Eliot's guide is to be used for early readings and forgotten when no longer needed. Here, Hough suggests, Eliot tells us how to read *The Waste Land* and, if we do, the explanation works – in places. The opening twenty lines can be seen as elliptical narrative, but can one speak of the logic of the imagination when Pound did certain things to the poem? Hough argues that the problems raised by the structure of *The Waste Land* have not been faced: structure has been a matter of attack or defence. Unity has been found in the theme of disillusionment, the fragmentary nature of modern life, or prompted by notes which refer to Jessie Weston, but, if we stand back, the mixed modes, the diverse styles simply do not cohere. If criticism has connected things thematically (or by analogy with music), the objects, persons and ideas should relate to one another and they do not. Shorn of paraphrasable sense, of all narrative or discursive line, the poem relies on the play of contrasted images alone. This gives it, Hough concedes, a startling concentration and brilliance, but it is a method adequate only for very short poems and very special effects such as depictions of dreams or states of madness. Hough has a point, though whether he has made it persuasively enough is a matter of taste (or faith?); in the larger expanse of his argument his actual detail often seems trivial.

More compelling is David Craig's complaint (1960) about defeatism in *The Waste Land*. Craig sees the poem as an outstanding example of a work which offered a defeatist personal depression in the guise of a full, impersonal picture of society and encouraged in its readers a superior cynicism, flattering the reader as a 'sole bearer of a fine culture which the new mass barbarians have spurned and spoiled'. Quoting from Leavis, Craig points to the assumption that the view of society and life in the poem is both self-evident and acceptable. If there are various techniques, one in particular stands out, and that is the running on from one area of experience, place, time or social class to another. Thus in part II he finds the so-called irony little more than ordinary sarcasm. The women are made so sour and unlovely that we have the strong feeling of the poet's superiority bolstered by references to a past that embodied a way of life that was better – a view pessimistic readers can share. The poet's meaning is clear: modern civilisation spoils what was once 'gracious, lovely, ceremonious, and natural'. Craig admits that it is actually a bit more complicated than that, but he still insists that history and reality are being manipulated to 'fit an escapist kind of prejudice'. He wonders why critics faced with a comparison between old times and a view of contemporary life that is 'impossible, pointless or else feasible only by specific fields and not overall' should surrender (as do Leavis, Wilson, Kenner) to a desparing view of civilisation. There are, after all, two ways of looking at the Industrial Revolution: defeatist and constructive. The outlook which assumes the fineness of the older culture belongs to the defeatist class. Village life was socially healthy in some ways but narrow and cruel in others, and, though the anti-human effects of industrial labour were perceived by Marx (passages from *Das Kapital* are cited), he saw it also as a means of winning through to the *new* good life. *The Waste Land* mobilises only negative responses. Craig's real objections emerge, however, only at the end of the article, where he detects reactionary politics (shared by Eliot and Leavis); these are most clearly visible in part v. Craig notes that when the poem was being written 'the civilized armies of Britain, America, France and Japan were invading Russia on twenty-three fronts'.

Eliot has never been a favourite of the Left. He was, in Ernest Bates's telling phrase, the Leisure Class Laureate, a member of that impotent degenerate class which oppresses the workers (*Modern Monthly*, 7 Feb 1933). He displays a most un-American elitism. John Strachey, in *The Coming Struggle for Power* (1932, 1934), argued that the 'whole capitalist world is on its way to barbarism', and that not only the working class but any man or woman of sense must realise that we cannot retain both capitalism and civilisation. For him, Eliot in *The Waste Land* had given a vivid portrayal of the reactions of a sensitive man 'to the decay of the whole system of society into which he has been born'. It is the most considerable poem produced in English in our day and expresses 'the whole agonizing disintegration of an old and once strong social system with the greatest poignancy'. Published in 1922, it was, therefore, written at the 'most acute point of the postwar crisis of capitalism', though Strachey also notes a personal side – the typical New England Puritan 'lamenting delicately over lost opportunities' – and strands that foreshadow the mystical solution which Eliot found to his own and society's problems. But the dominant impression is one of 'current social decay'. Strachey disclaims any pretence at writing literary criticism, directing his readers to consult Max Eastman. Eastman (1931) gives his study of the literary mind an ominous sub-title: 'Its Place in an Age of Science'. Claiming that science is now advancing into fields hitherto occupied by literature, having displaced magic, religion and abstract philosophy as a source of help and guidance, Eastman sees Eliot (and Pound) as prime movers in the 'vain last effort to be at once intellectual and ignorant of science'. For science suggests changes which a well-placed patrician will not welcome. Thus we have the Cult of Unintelligibility. Eastman notes that in *The Waste Land* there are references in seven languages, and quotations which are not from well-known English classics but from writers 'known only to the cognoscenti'. Eliot calls this civilising, but its effect is to narrow the circle of communication to 'a small group of specialists in a particular type of learning', and, though readers can look up the references, what they have enjoyed is 'a cerebral exercise rather than the emotional and intellectual experience of the poem' (p. 71). Why, Eastman

asks, do critics praise what they do not understand? Thus, as
a scientific experiment, he has *The Waste Land* 'explained' to
him by Joseph Wood Krutch, I. A. Richards and Merrill
Moore, who give him three directly opposed views, leaving
him to wonder if he should be impressed when a fourth critic
tells him that the poem means something else. Of course,
under this kind of experiment Eastman has probably
eliminated masterpieces from English literature completely,
but his charges of ignorance of science and social snobbery
remain. The poem is exclusive.

We need not share Craig's politics (or those of Strachey)
to recognise that *The Waste Land* is inadequate if seen as
general social diagnosis. For many readers the protagonist
was representative and the poem's view of life familiar, but
the poem is certainly rich enough to evoke multiple responses.
Craig at least reminds us that, if the poem is something more
than a personal grouse, it is something less than the Poem
For Our Times – though for such a critic as Harvey Gross
that is precisely what it is and the prophetic nature of the
poem has been fulfilled. Gross (1971) takes his title from
'Gerontion', and his chapter on Eliot incorporates his article
'"Gerontion" and the Meaning of History' (*PMLA*, June
1958, pp. 199–204). The thread that joins his authors together
is that their works may all be interpreted 'as a body of
prophetic knowledge', and the source books for this argument
are Hegel's *Philosophy of History* (which raised 'belief in the
reality of historical process to a metaphysical imperative')
and the works of his opponent Nietzsche, who embraced the
idea of an end to the process, the Apocalypse. Thus what
Gerontion knows is the downfall of Europe, with little hope
for spiritual rebirth, and the poem offers us 'philosophic
pessimism . . . anti-semitism, Nietzschean *amor fati*' and a
glimpse of political programmes in the coming era (Gross
1971, p. 42). Eliot cautions us, however, that the views of his
'hero' are only tentative and may be the product of a
disordered mind. The prophetic nature of *The Waste Land*
needs no comment: what was nightmare is now reality.
What, then, after fifty years, is the poem about? Gross sees it
as a mirror and a window, and the chief spectator at the
window is the prophet Tiresias, who is 'the enlarged and
multiplied persona of Gerontion' (p. 45). His suffering

consciousness unites the poem in which the historical process has all but stopped: history waits 'and nothing happens'.

Gross supports his historical interpretation by noting that, while Eliot's copy of Jessie Weston has some uncut pages and appears not to have been studied deeply, his copy of Hegel is heavily annotated and has obviously been read from cover to cover. Since Eliot was a student of philosophy, this is perhaps not surprising. While it is true that four years of war are behind the poem ('"That dirty war" and an enervating peace have rendered men either impotent or brutally lustful and women either hysterical or frigidly acquiescent' – p. 55), one wonders if the connection is entirely just. Some details are worrying in the climate of sexuality Gross finds in the poem. The influence of Wagner is definitely there, but to describe *Tristan and Isolde* and *Parsifal* as decadent ('*Tristan and Isolde*, which tells an overheated tale of love and death; and *Parsifal*, which makes a plea for Aryan racial purity in the ambience of a Black Mass' – p. 51) is only one way of putting it.

Gross suggests, also, that we must read 'myth' here as something more than a sub-plot about the Grail; myth means 'a meta-historical search for meaning in human events', and *The Waste Land* suspends us between two major myths which explain the shape of the historical process, both presented in religious terms: the Christian explanation and that of cyclical Eastern religions. The downfall of Europe (hooded hordes and maternal lamentation) produces not pessimism but, rather, new hopes. Cultural renewal may come from familiar sources (both the gods of the fertility cults and the God of Israel came from Asia), while the Cumean Sybil recalls a time when the Roman Empire was unsuccessfully struggling to repel forces that were apparently destructive but which were, ultimately, forces for 'spiritual renewal and historical rebirth'. There is some irony, remembering Craig's strictures about part v, in finding that, according to Gross, Eliot was actually welcoming the new life from the East!

More useful, perhaps, bearing those strictures in mind, might be the approach of Roger Kojecký (1971). He admits that Eliot's reputation as a critic of society does not stand high and decided to put the record straight by actually looking at what Eliot said and when. Obviously this kind of study is at its best after Eliot had become an Anglo-Catholic, and a characteristic Anglican concern for the relationship between Church and State came to dominate his writing. Eliot moved into drama after all as a way of bringing poetry to a larger public and involving a greater variety of people in a poetic event which contrasts with the elitist nature often attributed to *The Waste Land*. But of that poem Kojecký notes that it appears to have begun in the poet's mind (in language and subject) on a lower social stratum. The first section, for example, originally began with an account of a night out spent in various low places in London (*sic*) recalled the morning after. The public house and the typist–clerk incidents remained in the poem, but as it evolved it was given form, Kojecký believes, with anthropological perspectives from Eliot's reading of writers such as Weston and Frazer, and so became a more sophisticated attempt at capturing a modern urban consciousness refracted and projected 'through a figure as impersonal as the brooding Tiresias'.

Cross-roads

C. B. Cox (1970), looking at two passages from *The Waste Land* which Brooks 'explained' in terms of paradox, comments that such an explanation is really a simplification, giving the poem an unsuitable allegorical meaning, since what happens is not paradox but contradiction. And even such a word as 'contradiction' – suggesting as it does some balance of opposing ideas – is wrong, just as using such a word as 'protagonist' disturbs Cox, who in using it contradicts the doubts he has whether such a creature really exists. The note on Tiresias shows Eliot's uncertainty, that he wanted the poem to have what it does not have – a presiding consciousness. Citing Kenner (on Bradley) and Wolheim (on Eliot at Harvard), Cox suggests that *The Waste Land* does not proceed towards clarification but rather groups together different or opposing views which may exist in one mind supposing – and Eliot is profoundly sceptical on this – that any individual could be a coherent entity. Contradiction, then, in poetry before Eliot's conversion reflects his concern to collect points of view rather than judge between them, in a form that conveys uncertainty about personality, the relationship between words and objects, between words and his own consciousness. Cox's analysis of the poem concludes that Eliot's intention was to prevent the reader from accepting any particular point of view. *The Waste Land* is alive with 'the possibility of form', but as we read it we are aware of various kinds of structure and method, each of which breaks down; such criss-cross effects prevailed until Eliot could write poetry based on the eternal presence of Christ.

Possibly Cox overstates the virtues of incoherence, but at least he tells us that the way to read the poem is to see how the words work together and 'not fight desperately to find an ordered narrative'. But John Peter's objections and his desire to find a thread for readers remain. Pound certainly provided one such thread, though the author of *The Cantos* was not particularly troubled by form! According to Ackroyd (1984), Pound *rescued* the poetry by imposing order on it. In the original version, Ackroyd notes, Eliot had developed his gift for dramatic impersonation and allusiveness (the title 'He Do the Police in Different Voices' reminds us that Eliot was an accomplished mimic and parodist), but Pound refused to see Eliot's scheme and handed us the poem we have now, which – since Eliot's own context has been removed – requires us to provide a context of our own: so the poem can be seen as autobiography, the account of a collapsing society, an allegory of the Grail or a Buddhist meditation (p. 120). In Eliot's reviews we encounter a variety of voices under a variety of names – 'Crites', 'T. S. Apteryx', 'Gus Krutzsch' – but, if the role of the poet was to play possum, most critics agree that, however various the statements, they are recognisably the product of a single mind and the voice is always that of Eliot. Moreover, when he was writing 'St Sebastian' he was also working on the epic of King Bolo (and still writing it in 1927), for which Behr's description is 'mildly obscene'. Contradiction in his life and work is everywhere, the clash, as Ronald Bush (1984) sees it, between romantic yearning and intellectual detachment. The unity in Eliot's work and *The Waste Land* is that unity of inspiration which Eliot praised in his essay on Jonson.

This admittedly vague concept challenges the more careful pattern which, say, Elisabeth Schneider (1975) argues for.

She claims that Eliot was inspired by what Wilson Knight had done for Shakespeare in *The Wheel of Fire* (1930), for which Eliot wrote the introduction. Borrowing a phrase from Henry James – 'the figure in the carpet' – Eliot noted that the pattern in Shakespeare was elaborate and inscrutable and stated a preference for Dante, for a clear philosophical pattern (Christian and Catholic), but he was impressed by the way in which Wilson Knight considered Shakespeare's work as a whole. Our first duty, Eliot suggested, was to grasp the whole design and consider character and plot in our 'understanding of this subterrene or submarine music'. But, as Bush points out, Schneider's argument overlooks other influences (e.g. Mallarmé) and ignores what moved Eliot in Knight's account: namely, that Shakespeare not merely reworked his themes but that in the romances he reworked tragedy into something more happy. In 1929 Eliot was painfully receptive to the hope that this offered. *The Waste Land* was written in the context of his father's death and his mother's visit, both of which were painful experiences; and, Bush reminds us, Tiresias is part of the Oedipus story, whose hero kills his father and sleeps with his mother. Bush's analysis of the poem proceeds from these premises and suggests that the unity of inspiration attributed to Jonson becomes Eliot's own way of binding together fragments, images drawn from nightmares. We should not, Bush argues, pay too much attention to the sources, because Eliot wishes us to attend not to his models but to his mood (1984, p. 38): what he borrowed was other people's feelings rather than quotations that would make ironic comment. Images from other writers served the same purpose as images from life: they were bits of an objective world uncontaminated by Eliot's personality or style, but borrowing from books also suggested that the speaker (Prufrock, Gerontion and finally the speaker in *The Waste Land*) was avoiding life and borrowing feeling rather than suffering it. What allusion showed was learning. Bush feels that Eliot's original poem did not sufficiently conceal what Eliot had done, and he gave it to Pound for alteration. In fact, Pound altered very little, and so Eliot turned to a technique he thought he had observed in Joyce: the mythic method. Bush, therefore, agrees with most critics that Weston and Frazer were superimposed at the very end; that the title and what seems to be, from the notes, the controlling myth of the Grail legend (impersonal, social) introduced the possibility of character, plot and ideas which continue to obscure the lyrical centre (personal and felt) of the poem. But the reader is in some difficulty here, as Bush's own allusion to Tiresias as a character in the Oedipus story suggests. The allusions, we are told, are borrowed feeling, mood not model, but does this not require us to know the models in some way so as to know the mood?

The knowledge of such sources brings us to Grover Smith, whose study 'in Sources and Meanings' appeared in 1956. Smith analyses poems and plays, examining such sources as can be identified and looking at the ideas behind each work and those literary echoes which enrich meaning. The second edition (1974) noted that, since Eliot's death, the biographical emphasis had gained ground, intensified by the publication of the facsimile edition (1971), and that speculation had focused on Eliot's first marriage. In the main Grover Smith still felt that biography was outside the scope of his book, but he noted the lack of compassion in Eliot's poetry whenever Vivienne figures in it. There is, he points out, 'profuse testimony to Eliot's misery, none to hers' – a fact that biographers will have to reckon with. As far as *The Waste Land* is concerned, this study is superseded by *The Waste Land* (1983), and in the Preface he returns to the dangerous but inevitable biographical aspects of the poem. He reminds us that the personal nature of the poem had always been clear (citing Mary Hutchinson's comment recorded in Virginia Woolf's diary [23 June 1922] that it was 'Tom's autobiography – a melancholy one') but that in Eliot's lifetime comment on it would be considered too personal. Smith also notes the circular nature of biographical interpretation, in which the poem is used to interpret a life in such a way as to confirm the desired reading of the poem.

Looking at the two epigraphs for the poem (Conrad deleted, Petronius substituted), he suggests that they show the two aspects of the poem: the Conrad (from *The Heart of Darkness*) was personal, introspective, recalling a work that showed the ruined wasted life of a man of high ideals 'who had fallen into degradation and who lies dying with a vision of himself', while the Petronius was mythological and captures the significance of a life 'that cannot let go of its agony and find death' (Smith 1983, p. xiii). The single-volume treatment of *The Waste Land* allows Grover Smith to incorporate material recently available and place the poem in a more spacious context, reminding us that the poem has two kinds of importance: the historical and the poetical. Originally, after all, *The Waste Land* was simply a poem which became a historical event and a cultural monument. Originally, too, it was either a hoax or, which was worse, a poem with a social meaning that was detestable. Thus Eliot in 1931 was obliged to reject the idea that he was expressing the disillusion of a generation, though he qualified the rejection later by remarking (in 'Virgil and the Christian World') that, though a poet's lines 'may be for him only a means of talking about himself without giving himself away', those secret feelings may, ultimately, express the 'exultation or despair of a generation'.

The feelings in the poem were Eliot's, but Grover Smith sees them as transformed in ways he explores in chapter 2 of his book. Smith believes that Eliot presented himself in relation to the past (tradition), but its significance rested on what happened to it in him (individual talent). The key word is 'transformation' – both of the past (sources and allusions) and of his personal feelings. In writing *The Waste Land*, Eliot sought to emulate the metaphysical poets whose sensibility could devour any kind of experience. Smith examines Eliot's reading and writing at the time before moving on to the idea of structure (and myth). He then considers the effect of the facsimile edition and the notes. Eliot's views on the notes are contradictory: to counter the charge of plagiarism or to fill out a volume that was 'inconveniently short'. They may be 'a remarkable exposition of bogus scholarship' now stuck to the poem, and they may have stimulated 'the wrong kind of interest' and sent so many readers off on a wild-goose chase. But what, Eliot could be asked, would be the right kind of interest? Eliot co-operated, after all, with John Hayward when he compiled supplementary notes for the French translation (1947), and approved the lot.

Grover Smith is correct in suggesting that without the sources we cannot grasp that extra dimension of inherited tradition with which the poem is involved, though the danger of confusing the sources with the poetry is ever-present. Smith writes short essays on key images (e.g. the Tarot pack – its use was 'as prankish as serious'), reminding us, at the end, that, since there is such an incomplete correlation between sources and allusions recognised or in the notes and the actual sources and models, we should always be aware of the playfulness noted by, say, Stanley Sultan (1977).

Smith's final chapter considers the critical reception of the poem since 1922, providing in one short book (170 pages) as much as any reader could want to explain or justify the strong emotions aroused by a series of lyrical fragments called *The Waste Land*.

ASH WEDNESDAY

We have our inheritance.

Transitional

For Frank Kermode (1967), 'to have Eliot's great poem [i.e. *The Waste Land*] in one's life involves an irrevocable but repeated act of love'. It was a poem that aroused passions, admiring or otherwise, in a way that *Ash Wednesday* did not. D. S. Savage (1944) is not alone in seeing Eliot's poetic career from 1925 as one of deterioration. As he had grown older the moralist had developed at the expense of the aesthete, and there is a 'pronouncedly religiose strain' in poems up to and including *The Hollow Men*. Savage sees the difference between the early and later poetry as one of environment: the early Eliot is recognisable for his personal presentation of urban squalor and its soiled humanity, and for the conviction this presentation carries, whereas the later poetry is less concrete 'because of its intellectual rather than sensuous nature'. Eliot, trying to achieve the generalised image, only creates the concrete by using archaic or biblical imagery 'which is literary rather than actual', while the weariness, boredom and self-doubt which was mastered and made significant occur in the later poems only unintentionally, because they come from things the poem has failed 'to bring in subjection to his inspiration'.

Ash Wednesday is like *The Waste Land*, however, in one respect: both were poems created out of fragments and collected together under a single title. Eliot admitted in the *Paris Review* (1959) that that is the way his mind works – 'doing things separately and then seeing the possibility of fusing them together, altering them, and making a kind of whole of them'. But the whole here is undeniably (and, as Savage says, 'intensely') personal. Many readers would agree with W. H. Pritchard (1980) that in none of Eliot's other poems do we occupy such a 'strained position' watching 'certain private impulses attempt to find satisfactory expression in various scenes, images and verse forms' (p. 193).

There will always be uncertainty about the religious nature of *The Waste Land*, but *Ash Wednesday* is obviously a religious poem, albeit a transitional one. The following scenario will explain its genesis. At some time after 1923 (the year after *The Waste Land* was published), Eliot was introduced to William F. Stead, an ex-diplomat who had taken holy orders, and Stead encouraged Eliot to read seventeenth-century Anglican writers, particularly Lancelot Andrewes. In 1926 an unsigned article on Andrewes appeared, including passages that Eliot remoulded into 'The Journey of the Magi' (1927), and it was this poem – the first of a series later called 'Ariel Poems' – which 'released the stream' that led to *Ash Wednesday* (*New York Times Book Review*, 29 Nov 1953). In 1927 Eliot was baptised and confirmed in the Anglican Church and published 'Salutation' (part II of *Ash Wednesday*). 'Perchio non spero' (part I) appeared in 1928 and was followed in 1929 by 'Som de l'Escalina' (part III). Eliot also published *Dante* in the Faber 'Poets on Poets' series. *Ash Wednesday* was finally published on 24 April 1930.

The religious poet

Few readers at the time saw *The Waste Land* as a religious poem; most with some justice saw it as the disillusionment of a generation that was lost and Eliot's reception into the Anglican Church came as a shock (and for some as a betrayal), but, in retrospect, the continuity and personal nature of Eliot's work now seems obvious. As Hugh Kenner and many others pointed out, the image of the staircase in 'Som de l'Escalina' (1929) had appeared in 'Portrait of a Lady' (1910), where the first of a long series of characters mounts the stairs to a lady. This recurring image, Kenner suggests, is one of 'great inherent symbolic firmness' because it requires no explication, touching as it does on such situations as the unwilling suitor, the squalor of modern life, the unattainable mistress or a lady of contemplation (1959, p. 25). Kenner elsewhere (*Hudson Review*, 1949) regretted that the discussion of Eliot's poetry was 'bedevilled by its notorious separability into "earlier" and "later"', which, in fact, only means that Eliot changed his admirers, not his view, and enjoyed a succession of reputations. Eliot, Kenner insists, never changed his preoccupation (an 'intense concern with moral states') and his poetry is 'a developing action'. *Ash Wednesday* did alter criticism in one way, however. Grover Smith (1983) is correct when he reminds us that, if, during his lifetime, critics mainly stayed away from sensitive personal topics, Eliot's conversion provided a link between the cultural situation in *The Waste Land* and the private situation. But the result was unfortunate, for religion is clearly 'not in the poem but in the future of the poem'. *Ash Wednesday*, in particular, signalled possibilities and the personal note began to sound in Eliot criticism.

Certainly Eliot's shift from the satiric observation in such a poem as 'The Hippopotamus' or despair in *The Waste Land* required some explanation, and mainly the explanation was in terms of retrospective readings of the poems. Christian meaning was easy to find in such a poem as 'Gerontion', and *The Waste Land*, as we have seen, acquired religious overtones fairly easily. The determination to make Eliot a religious poet reaches its climax in Felix Clowder's (presumably) satiric article on *Old Possum's Book of Practical Cats* (1939). Old Deuteronomy is, clearly, the Established Church, while the Jellicle Cats are evangelicals, whose enthusiasm is to be deplored. The three names of a cat – the third of which is always hidden – obviously recalls the Trinity, and the fact that the Hebrew name of God was considered ineffable!

Whether Eliot shifted or developed may just depend on the choice of words. Eliot, in fact, published very little poetry between *The Waste Land* and becoming an Anglican, but Bush (1984) looks at the eight lectures delivered at Cambridge in

1926 on metaphysical poetry, which show Eliot changing his stance (p. 88ff.), responding to Dante and the *Vita Nuova*[1] and rejecting Laforgue and Donne, whose irony now seems only the 'disillusionment of immaturity'. The emphasis is now not on feeling but on the 'pattern which we make of our feelings', based on Dante's view that adolescent feelings should be reshaped by mature reflection. If, as Bush admits, the result lacks the intensity of *The Waste Land*, it nevertheless matched what was happening in Eliot's own life – his detachment (uncomfortably) from marriage, Faber instead of the bank, and entry into the Anglican Church: so Lancelot Andrewes rather than John Donne (and their sermons in both cases) and the problem of belief in poetry and literature. This is usually discussed (and Eliot does discuss it) in terms of the effect of a reader's convictions on his response. But the more interesting question, surely, is how far such considerations affected the texture of Eliot's own writing, and Bush's answer is that they affected it a great deal. Eliot's belief reshaped his views on diction and syntax, which make up the voice, the style of a poet, and which both 'involve the denotative aspects of language in a way that far exceeds the concerns of his earlier poetry', pointing him away from 'a poetry of pure or dramatic lyricism' towards 'a poetry of meditation' (p. 113). Bush notes that praise for Dryden grew between 1921 and 1930 – in 1921 Eliot showed little enthusiasm for the verse, though he was fascinated by the prose, but by 1930, when he delivered a series of five talks on Dryden for the BBC, he spoke of Dryden as one of the assured masters of English poetry, exhibiting good sense and propriety, which poetry cannot afford to do without. Such developments justify describing Eliot's later poetry as 'hard-won': it is an exclusive style and it is devotional poetry. And it was in 1927 that Eliot refuted I. A. Richards's claim that in *The Waste Land* he had effected a complete severance 'between poetry and *all* beliefs'. Later that year, in the *Dial*,

---

[1] The precise dating of Dante's works is impossible, but the first in order of composition was the *Vita Nuova* (1290–4), in which Dante collected thirty-one poems, most of which concern his love for Beatrice. These are linked by a prose narrative about that love which interprets the poems from the point of view of one who now sees that Beatrice was the instrument of his salvation.

he observed that the chief distinction of man is to glorify God.

For Lyndall Gordon (1977) there is no problem, since in her reading Eliot's life had always been a religious quest, from which he was distracted. She describes Eliot's mother as a kind of Dorothea Brooke, and his grandfather as a saintly man who taught that one must subordinate selfish interest to the good of the community and the Church, and who had journeyed to the mid-West to do just that. The idea of God abandoning man, of pilgrimage from imperfection to perfection, of the world as a waste land as a prerequisite to experiencing it in faith, were 'deeply rooted in Eliot's family and their Puritan past' (p. 94), though Unitarianism proved insufficient for Eliot's temperament. According to Gordon, Eliot was on the edge of conversion in 1914, and marriage was an alternative which failed. A series of poetic fragments culminates in *The Waste Land*, where Pound's editing blurred the pattern of exemplary lives (where there was always a dark night before conversion), bringing the cultural statement to the forefront. *The Waste Land* was the personal record of a man who saw himself as a candidate for the religious life but, because he was writing in an uncongenial age, chose to present his spiritual autobiography indirectly. Readers found a child of our time rather than a saint. *Ash Wednesday* and *Four Quartets* are simply more explicit.

The religious poem

In a letter to Stead (9 Aug 1930, quoted in Bush 1984, p. 131) Eliot wrote about the large area between poetry and 'devotional' verse that had not been explored by modern poets – 'the experience of a man in search of God, and trying to explain to himself his intenser human feelings in terms of the divine goal', which he had tried to do in *Ash Wednesday*. Written and published piecemeal as the poem was, the glue that held the bits together was neither myth nor narrative but personal, and the poem was originally dedicated to his wife, Vivienne, who might, Bush suggests, 'understand what he previously had not been able to put into words' (p. 132). The heart of the poem is Christian, though many readers feel that Eliot does not seem to be enjoying his faith. The questions to be asked of the poem were: Is it religious, or just Dante versified into English? If personal, is it not curiously detached? And what does it mean? And in answer to this last question (Eliot foresaw the danger) critics sympathetic to religion tend to leave us with piety rather than illumination.

The initial publication was so prodigal of paper that, after turning nearly seven empty pages (as one critic observed), the phrase 'Because I do not hope to turn again' took on immediate meaning. It was, as Eastman (1931) sardonically remarked, expensive poetry. Contemporary reviews, nevertheless, show a respectful response. Gerald Heard (*Week-End Review*. 3 May 1930)* wondered, since this was religious poetry, which tradition Eliot was in: the native English tradition, where religion was not a mystery to be shown through symbol and ritual but rather 'sanctified common-sense' or the iconographic tradition, where words can only be images not argument, since that is the only way to reach the infinite. Francis Birrell (*Nation and Athenaeum*, 31 May 1930)* noted that satire and wit had been replaced here by beauty, but, however beautiful the poem might be, he wished he knew what it all meant. Are the images liturgical and mystical (and he ought to know about them) or merely 'private associations in the sensibility of Mr Eliot', in which case can they mean anything? Edmund Wilson (*New Republic*, 20 August 1930)* found the poem less brilliant, the imagery less vivid (because more 'artificial') but admired Eliot's ability to put the right words (with none to spare) in the right order, making the poem a not unworthy successor to *The Waste Land*. But Morton D. Zabel (*Poetry*, Sep 1930)* thought that Eliot would perplex readers by going back to that absolutism of which 'The Hippopotamus' was 'an inverted parody, the "Sunday Morning Service" a social indictment, "Gerontion" a broken and pathetic echo, and the chorus of "The Hollow Men" a derisive denial'. What was present in all Eliot's work, however, was the sense that he had never been able to cut the roots of his native Puritanism, which bound him to the soil of Christianity. But, where the

* An asterisk indicates that the material is reprinted in *T. S. Eliot: The Critical Heritage*, ed. Michael Grant (1982).

emotional adventures of the early poetry were viewed with clear-eyed self-scrutiny, here Zabel found only 'a desultory kind of allegory'. Thomas Moult (*Bookman*, Sep 1930)* thought *Ash Wednesday* had not been written for the plain man, and those who sought to find plain meanings in it did so at their peril. If Eliot had returned from a voyage of discovery to write about the need for faith, it was a faith 'dressed in austere colours', while for William Rose Benét (*Saturday Review*, 18 Oct 1930)* *Ash Wednesday* was another dose of despair with a rather hopeless appeal to religion and the injunction to sit still, which he could not see the point of. If we can admire the music of the poem, Benét urged us, we should ignore the disillusionment, which approaches mere apathy.

Allen Tate (*Hound and Horn*, Jan–Mar 1931)* tackled the difficulties positively. The reasoning he detects in many readers is that, since Anglo-Catholicism will not do for them, poetry written under its spell must be less valuable: to accept the poetry is to accept an invitation to join the Anglican Church. Tate feels that the idea that a poem is *so personal* that it is useless overlooks the technique, which, if less obvious than the irony of *The Waste Land*, still justifies the poet's search for humility. Eliot's failure to understand his position is irony, but the insight into that failure is humility, and Eliot's ability to give us freshness by using the trite justifies our seeing *Ash Wednesday* as the only valid religious poetry of today.

F. R. Leavis (1932) could say, then, without a hint of contradiction, that here Eliot's concern is specifically religious. He concedes that *Ash Wednesday* is a difficult poem, because its rhythms establish 'a special order of experience, dedicated to spiritual exercises', yet at the same time exhibit the same self-exploration and self-scrutiny. The poetical problem here is also a spiritual problem, and the absence of punctuation warns us against crude interpretation (that is, trying to find in the poem anything in the nature of a prose statement): we have to take the poem as a whole, since it works by 'compensations, resolutions, residuums and convergences'. Thus, if the general effect of part I, renunciation, is negative, the formula ('Teach us to sit still') registers 'a positive religious impulse'. In part II it is common to ask who the

Lady is and what the three white leopards stand for. The Lady's identity, Leavis suggests, need not bother us: she reminds us of various ladies and helps to define 'the mode of religious contemplation that characterizes the poem'. Here Leavis recalls Eliot's comment (in his *Dante*) that when Dante encounters a lady named Matilda her identity 'need not at first bother us' – where the crucial phrase is Eliot's 'at first'! Certainly the theme of *Ash Wednesday* is death, and death means extinction; and certainly the effect is different from, say, the use of that theme in *The Hollow Men*. The difference is that here it becomes something positive and it becomes positive by association with the Lady and a specific religious tradition, an association assisted by the rhythms and tone of the poem. Some knowledge, however, of that tradition and that liturgy would seem to be helpful. Similarly Leavis insists that the white leopards need no interpretation. They act 'directly' to reinforce 'the effect of ritual we have noted' and to suggest the 'mode of experience, the kind of spiritual exercise', to which the poem is devoted as the formal quality of the verse (with its echoes of ritual and liturgy) helps to define the plane on which the poem works. Leavis is arguing that the spiritual discipline and the poetic are one and the same and, therefore, the poem is accessible. Thus the 'stairs' in part III will recall, for the reader who knows Dante, the stairs in *Purgatorio* (a reminiscence confirmed in part IV) but for other readers they will work directly. They will suggest a hard climb upwards, with meetings on the stairs and views from windows as the poet climbs. Here Eliot blends the reminiscent (literary or liturgical) with the 'immediately evocative'. But the view from the window in part III (at the first turning of the third stair) which seemed to be a distraction becomes, in part IV, a source of refreshment where the lady (still unspecified) goes in white and blue: 'in Mary's colour'. Here the poet may be remembering an actual religious experience or recalling a time when the symbolism was fresh, when Dante's Beatrice was his salvation both as a poet and a man. But, Leavis points out, the modern poet cannot have Dante's certitude nor his 'higher dream' – we have forgotten the trick, Eliot says, and can no more recapture Dante's way of looking at things than we can recapture his belief. The base for rejoicing in part IV is, for

Eliot and his readers, precarious and brings doubt and fear in part v. These doubts develop and the poem ends on a despairing recognition of the 'equivocal'. But this doubt in the last poem also becomes part of the spiritual discipline which fosters humility and ambiguity: things lost because the heart rebels and gives in to temptation, and things lost with regret (i.e. questioning the renunciation). If *Ash Wednesday* lacks the richness and range of *The Waste Land*, Leavis finds it nevertheless remarkable because of 'the strange and difficult regions of experience' it explores.

Similarly Spender (1975) finds *Ash Wednesday* remarkable because the 'I' of the poem is not, as previously, either aesthetic or conditioned by the state of civilisation, nor representative of a state of consciousness, but the naked self in the presence of God. This speaker is no longer involved with the world but abandons hope and the things that go with hope (personal ambition, the struggle for personal happiness or caring about civilisation), so that we have a sense of the burden falling away to be replaced by a new responsibility: prayer. Prayer has two aspects – prayer for oneself and one's life in eternity, and prayer for one's neighbour; hence 'I' and 'we' can be used throughout the poem. For Spender, prayer is both subject and hero of the poem, connecting despair and hope, belief and unbelief. The least successful (because the most difficult) section is part v, where the subject is the relationship between word and Word (where, we could say, the poetic and spiritual problems connect most acutely). The Word is the word made Flesh, the Incarnation which is the end of the quest that Spender sees as the theme of all Eliot's work up to *Ash Wednesday*. The Word as a symbol is unlike other symbols in poetry, since in it the supremely poetic idea coincides with the greatest mystery. Spender believes that accepting the truth of the Incarnation altered Eliot's attitude to poetry. Symbols can be used without believing in them, as material for poetry, but the Word symbol must be believed in and must find words to express Itself. In this poem the poet still struggles with unbelief and to find words for the Word.

So, though Conrad Aiken (*Poetry*, Dec 1934) saw *Ash Wednesday* as perhaps 'the most beautiful of all Mr Eliot's poems' and with a value that may outlast *The Waste Land*, many also saw it as the beginning of a diminution of vigour and variousness. The circle has narrowed and after this poem it goes on narrowing. And certain views emerge. The most prominent is the clash between personal and impersonal poet. The poem is clearly about Eliot, but he has made himself very distant from it. That distance may represent the traditional poet in contradiction to the personal poet, but it gives the poem an air of remoteness.

The impersonal–personal poet

Ash Wednesday is written in the first person and appears to recount a personal experience, but, as Bush (1984) points out, since Eliot wishes to emphasise the universal nature of that personal experience, he takes great pains not to dramatise the personal flavour of the speaking voice; like Lancelot Andrewes, he effaces personal feeling. A romantic temperament as strong as Eliot's continues, however, to make itself felt, and the poet, striving for prose-like precision, achieves neither emotional nor discursive clarity: only sonority. But this sonority, 'along with the extraordinary power of the truncated vision that escapes the censure of Eliot's discipline, suggests something has been repressed that will not stay repressed for long' (p. 136). The 'I' and the voices that it produces which are 'mine' imply a belief that something in the self is substantial and will survive dismemberment – something not present in *The Waste Land*. Bush also notes that there are two endings – the first about guarding the will in the sanctuary of 'this pool' and ambivalent about remaining in such confines, and the published ending, in which, short of death, no sanctuary is possible and Eliot confirms a willingness to carry on the battle between God and the world indefinitely, an assertion ebullient enough (in Bush's estimation) to keep the poem from being, in A. D. Moody's phrase, 'just as life-denying as it can be'.

Kenner's 'Invisible Poet' (1959) is clearly present in *Ash Wednesday*, where a new style (language open, even tranquil, with lapses into small talk) produces a loss of vigour because there is a withdrawal from individual speech. Eliot's poetry

is now related less to the speaking voice and more to the
'renovated decorums of the impersonal English language'
(p. 225). Kenner admires the tension produced in the poem
by nouns, verbs and adjectives pulling two ways: the heart
lost to the world and lost in the world, a tension expressed in
the phrase, 'Teach us to care and not to care'. And, if the *stil
nuovo*, unpunctuated, was never spoken anywhere in the
world, it is never remote from 'the constructions (if not the
energies) of actual speech' (p. 229). Kenner also notes an
'insistent mellifluousness' that recalls Tennyson and unites
Ash Wednesday with *The Waste Land* by way of Tennyson in
themes of quester, Chapel Perilous, elusive visions associated
with a lady and thence, by way of Dante, gathering divinity.
The quest in *Ash Wednesday* is to arrive at a knowledge of the
possibilities of temporal redemption 'sufficient to prevent our
being deluded by a counterfeit of the negative way' (p. 235),
and the centre of perception that goes on the journey in the
poem, the 'I', is a focal point 'as specific as an "I" can be,
but too wholly absorbed in its own spiritual states to be
called a protagonist' (p. 226).

E. E. Duncan Jones (1947) sees the poem as about the
penitential aspect of the spiritual life (as the title insists)
beginning with self-exploration and self-examination. Such
terms obviously prepare us for a personal poem, yet
throughout his sympathetic analysis Duncan Jones refers
consistently to the 'I' of the poem and nowhere feels the need
to say 'Eliot'. When at the end he notes that 'the poet faces
the sea', the word 'poet' comes as a shock; the 'I' of the
poem, Duncan Jones suggests, is 'not so much a personality
as a will', and, in keeping with such impersonality, the
poetry 'at its peaks and climaxes ... passes into the
anonymous language of the Church'.

Exegesis

Since the 'anonymous language of the Church' is for most
readers another foreign language, it, like the allusions, will
need some explanation. Duncan Jones (1947), while admitting
that there are frequent references to Dante and other writers,
suggests that we need not recognise them (though if we do

they will 'reinforce' some of the suggestions of the poem): *Ash Wednesday* is poetry that can communicate before it is understood. Though Eliot follows Dante in many ways, he does not limit his symbols as Dante does (or as the commentators have done for him). There is no narrative, though we can, with goodwill and the experience of Dante as a guide, 'disengage a "story" from the poem'. But, if Eliot had attached importance to narrative, he would have made it more prominent. The poem, then, is a sequence of images resting on that logic of the imagination described by Eliot in his preface to St-John Perse's *Anabasis* (1930).

Some critics have looked for a pattern in terms of the Mass. Carl Wooten (1961) finds the structure of the Mass 'loosely imposed on the whole poem', leaving us to wonder who imposed it and whether 'loosely' appears to cover difficulties in interpretation. Gwenn R. Boardman (1962) claims that the structure can be found in the Mass. As the title implies, we are on Ash Wednesday, whose Mass introduces the Lenten sequence which culminates in Easter. Eliot, she finds, has used not only the themes of the six Sundays, but also the two series of 'six' found in every Mass, and the sections of the poem parallel the six Remembrances and the six Acts. Paul J. Dolan (1967) sees the poem as a dramatic monologue about a man about to enter a new way of life: a catechumen. So the symbols in the poem are derived 'primarily' from what is still called the Mass of the Catechumens – the opening part after which the unbaptised had to leave. 'Primarily' because, as Dolan cheerfully admits, the phrase 'Lord I am not worthy' does not occur in the Mass of the Catechumens! But Eliot, we are told, was not obliged to provide us with a 'neat formula'. Such interpretations tend to make the poem too narrowly Christian (doctrinal) in a way Eliot seems to be trying to avoid. And the Mass to which Eliot would have referred is, anyway, now, like the Authorised Version of the Bible, not familiar to many readers: both sources are becoming as remote as Dante.

It was, of course, in his essay on Dante (1929) that Eliot advanced the view that the less he knew about the poet and his work before he began to read the better, leading to the notorious statement about poetry communicating before it is understood. It is better at the start not to know or care what

Dante's images mean, though Eliot conceded that enjoyment of the poetry will make us want to understand the meaning. In the Harvard lectures (1932–3) Eliot observed that the chief use of meaning was to keep the reader's mind diverted while 'the poem does its work on him' – much as the thoughtful burglar keeps a bit of meat for the house-dog.

Eliot seems to handle the problem of belief in a similarly casual fashion by pointing out that you are not called upon to believe what Dante believed – such belief will give the reader no more understanding. It may be easier for a Catholic to grasp the meaning than for the agnostic, but that is not because the Catholic believes – only because he has been instructed.

Dante, for Eliot, was the most comprehensive and 'most *ordered* presentation of emotions that has ever been made', and his relation to Dante has been considered by Mario Praz (1937) 'from an Italian point of view'. Matthiessen (1935) had pointed to a connection with Dante scholarship at Harvard, but Praz suggests that Ezra Pound was probably more influential with his power of bringing poets alive as contemporary, particularly in such a book as *The Spirit of Romance* (1910). Eliot attended classes on Dante at Harvard in 1906, and the 'dignified impersonality' of medieval writers is extolled in Grandgent's *Dante* (New York, 1916) – a book high on Eliot's list of works that influenced him. Indeed, Praz suggests that most of Eliot's characteristic precepts as a critic – his theory of the objective correlative and the impersonality of the poet – arose in connection with his study of Dante. In Santayana and Grandgent moral idealism and the dread of vulgarity (typical of the Puritan mind), and in Pound – *il miglior fabbro* – concern for the technique of poetry impressed upon Eliot the need to find 'a pattern of clear visual images capable of evoking immediately the underlying emotion' (Praz 1937, p. 534). Through references Praz defines the influence of Dante on Eliot as a strengthening of the tendency to use 'a language not different from the ordinary, and at the same time capable of philosophical turns, that he had found in his early model, Laforgue' (p. 537). The pattern of images in *Ash Wednesday* may be suggested by Dante but in an odd way – as if Eliot had been reading Dante without much caring about the meaning but letting himself be impressed by a few images which he then rearranged in his own mind – just as coloured glass in a kaleidoscope can give different (but harmonious) patterns (p. 543). Ackroyd (1984) describes Eliot's imagination as one which went to literature for that which life could not give – a sense of order – and Eliot turned to Dante as the embodiment of cultural and social order. When published in its final form, *Ash Wednesday* lost its five titles from Dante, but in it Eliot sought to imitate the way in which Dante, in the *Vita Nuova*, transformed a sexual event as a child into 'an intellectual and spiritual reality'. Both Unger (1966) and Williamson (1953) refer to the seminal nature of the *Vita Nuova*. Williamson had already used the book in his study of *The Waste Land* when he looked at 'Dans le Restaurant', whose conclusion, translated into English, forms part IV. In the French poem a rather dirty old waiter recalls his first sexual experience for a diner, an experience interrupted and regretted which connects with Dante's account in *Vita Nuova* (said to have taken place when he was nine, though Eliot doubted that it could have taken place as late as that). Williamson points out that the Ariel poems all reflect subjects significant to Eliot: exploring new experiences or extending an experience already begun. The subjects of these poems (the Bible – as in the story of the Magi or Simeon; Dante – the deflection of the will from God; and Shakespeare – the recovery of Marina) produce a story in themselves, but they are also typically Eliot because they are made contemporary. History is something which continues to happen. And we can see *Ash Wednesday* as a cluster of Ariel poems reminding us that, exiled from Eden, we return to dust, and working over two themes: turning from the word to God, and exile from God – drawn from Dante and the Scriptures used by Dante. Williamson feels that comparison with *The Waste Land* is instructive in other ways too – the treatment of women, for example. Woman now becomes the symbol of a more beneficent love, the attraction towards God. This is not a view that Pinkney (1984) agrees with. With some justice he suggests that what *Ash Wednesday* shows about women is the danger of idealisation and handing over guilt to ritual and the symbolism of Christianity. The result is a dualism that intensifies the distaste felt in *The Waste Land*: 'the Blessed Virgin so monopolises female virtue that it

becomes almost an act of public hygiene to "do in" the
women one comes across in daily life, so necessarily tainted
as these latter are' (p. 117).

Some critics, while acknowledging Dante and religion,
write for readers not deeply involved with either. Grover
Smith (1956) wonders why Eliot made his poem so cryptic.
His analysis refers to the sources (including Ash Wednesday
sermons preached by Lancelot Andrewes), and he reminds us
that the poem was dedicated to Vivienne Eliot, reunited with
her husband after a separation during 1926–8. The poem
had dramatic unity and a precise temporal focus provided by
the point of view of the protagonist. He can be compared
with Tiresias because he has a consistent point of view (even
if the consistency is despair) but he knows what Tiresias
cannot know – that salvation may require the negative
discipline of patience and denial 'not merely in the rejection
of carnality, but even in the loss of spiritual certitude'
(p. 137). Smith finds philosophical originality in the poem
because Eliot achieves a composite that both Dante and St
John of the Cross would have rejected. Because Eliot is
writing about exile he needs the analogy with the Dark Night
described by St John, but the negative mysticism of St John
would require Eliot to renounce the Lady as a spiritual
guide: St John would insist that she was a deterrent to
spiritual progress. In using Dante's affirmative pattern Eliot
'extinguishes' the Lady's identity, transferring it, symbolically,
to the Blessed Virgin – to such an extent that, as Grover
Smith admits, some will complain that she is so 'imperfectly
realized' that the feelings about her are drawn almost entirely
from Dantean allegory.

For most critics Ash Wednesday is clearly a transitional
poem that takes us out of The Waste Land into Four Quartets; it
is part of one long literary endeavour. Leonard Unger (1939)
insists that the movement from The Hollow Men to Ash
Wednesday was neither sudden nor abrupt. Indeed its roots
can be traced back in the prose as early as 1917. In this
retrospect The Waste Land must be considered as more
Christian than it originally appeared to be. The rocks, for
example, that are red in The Waste Land reappear as cool and
blue in Ash Wednesday, a deliberate strategy that illustrates
the unity of the Eliot canon. The Waste Land, Unger writes,

'*we can now see*' (emphasis added) looks forward to *Ash Wednesday*: setting one's land in order amounts to the 'practice of inner control', and *Ash Wednesday* shows that Eliot has been pursuing this resolution.

For Frye (1963), however, *Ash Wednesday* is a poem that looks forward and belongs with the later poems and five plays, all of which exhibit Eliot's ' "purgatorial" vision'. In the poem we have a desert, a garden and a stairway between them – images that have already appeared in ironic contexts (in what Frye labels the ' "infernal" vision', and usually connected with the failure of love); desert and garden are, of course, central symbols from our literary and religious heritage, and here Eliot has changed them slightly: thus, the desert which figures in the early poetry is now no longer sterile society but the meagre individual spiritual life. The narrator, in middle life, wishes to kill the ego and return it, on Ash Wednesday, to the dust whence it came, separating even the bones that cling together (so the leopards, if frightening, are also agents of redemption).

So there is much truth in Helen Gardner's comment that *Ash Wednesday* is not merely Eliot's most obscure poem but also the one most at the mercy of the temperaments and/or beliefs of the reader (1949, p. 122): one has only to consider what the critics do with those three leopards. Gardner is a good example of the synthetic critic, approaching the poem as part of the whole, remarking on style and imagery and coming down, finally, on the side of ambiguity. For Gardner *The Waste Land* ended with 'the truth of the human situation as the religious mind conceives it' (p. 98), and what is most noticeable in *Ash Wednesday* is the change in rhythms, style and imagery – the narrowing of the vision – and images drawn from dreams, not observation. These images are mostly beautiful, often drawn from nature (images in the earlier poems came from life lived in cities, and if from nature it was nature in its more sinister aspects), many of them traditional (rose, garden, fountain, desert, yew) but mingled with more esoteric images taken from medieval allegory (jewelled unicorns or white leopards). Where the earlier poetry was characterised by condensation – elliptical writing, omission of connecting phrases – *Ash Wednesday* is relaxed, repetitive, often incantatory, circling round phrases.

Thus Gardner suggests that a prose paraphrase of the earlier poetry would require expansion, but in many places in *Ash Wednesday* such a paraphrase would be shorter. *Ash Wednesday*, therefore, is undramatic, unrhetorical and lyrical, and the traditional symbols belong to the world of the lyric, where 'feeling seizes on the first image that comes to mind' and is stock. This change must, she allows, be connected with the fact that the author is a Christian while the author of *The Waste Land* was not, but the connection is complex. If faith is assumed in *Ash Wednesday* and the poem deals with the mortification of natural man, the themes of patience and aspiration seem, to Gardner, to be crossed by some sense of personal experience 'so painful that it can hardly be more than hinted at, and so immediate that it cannot be wholly translated into symbols' (p. 104). This gives each line an ambiguity which, she believes, 'it is not the critic's business to remove'. She also believes that it is a mistake to try and trace development from poem to poem, since the first three in the sequence appeared separately (and not in the order in which we now have them) and circle round the subject – aspiring to a state that can only be suggested through references to dreams or veiled figures and expressed mainly in language taken from the liturgy or the Bible 'and hardly at all in the poet's own words' (p. 114).

Eliot said that he had thought of adding to the poem, if it were to go into a second edition, some lines from Byron's *Don Juan*:

> Some have accused me of a strange design
>   Against the creed and moral of this land,
> And trace it in this poem, every line.
>   I don't pretend that I quite understand
> My own meaning when I would be *very* fine;
>   But the fact is that I have nothing planned
> Except perhaps to be a moment merry. . . .

But 'merry' is hardly the word most readers would apply to *Ash Wednesday*. F. O. Matthiessen (1935) sees in the later Eliot not merely Dante but also the Puritan mind of Hawthorne and Henry James. The religion posed a problem and he praised the Allen Tate review for sensibly summing it up: if Anglo-Catholicism does not satisfy, poetry written under its influence will not; the poem is not contemporary, it does not solve labour problems, it is special, personal and can do us no good. Matthiessen's answer is that the poem is best suited to the Eliotic audience that can neither read nor write. The poem impresses through the beauty of its sound, for here Eliot has summoned up all the resources of his 'auditory imagination' and the reader can feel the force of the poem 'long before his mind is able to give any statement of its "meaning"' (p. 115). Matthiessen concedes that it is clear Eliot would like to feel a more compelling faith than he does, but in our modern world it is difficult to find such belief.

Edmund Wilson (1931) had seen Eliot's conversion as a reawakening of the New Englander's conscience and consciousness 'of the ineradicable sinfulness of man', but Eliot, in spite of his meagre production, had become the leader of a generation because he had clearly been on his way somewhere, and the destination became plain in the new edition of *The Sacred Wood* (1928), where poetry was connected with morals and religion. The literary and conventional imagery upon which *Ash Wednesday* relies may be less vivid, but Wilson detected in the poem those qualities which made Eliot a remarkable poet: exquisite phrasing, mastery of metres, but, above all, that 'peculiar honesty' which Eliot praises in Blake.

Part Two: Appraisal

The problem

The duty of the presenter in such a review of criticism is to be impartial, to present as many ways of responding to the poems as possible without prejudice or comment. Such godlike impartiality is not, however, in human nature, nor is it, perhaps, particularly helpful. In deciding which responses are odd or downright daft, the presenter expresses an opinion in the critical debate and such decisions must be taken if the study is not to become comprehensive to the point of meaninglessness. But the problem is not merely one of achieving impartiality. If a wild-goose chase is distracting, it can also be fun, and deciding when some line of inquiry stops being a means and becomes an end can be difficult. For example: music. The analogy with music was encouraged by Eliot, who, after all, starts with a love song and moves to four quartets, but such a line of inquiry soon passes the point of usefulness. Indeed it is usually invoked to 'explain' why the poem should neither frighten nor puzzle us: here, like music, we are told, is poetry that can communicate before it is understood – which is often not particularly helpful to the reader to whom it has not communicated and who wants to know why not. Eliot's poetry is full of references to music, and a little Wagner is helpful in reading *The Waste Land*, but a critic such as Herbert Knust, in 'Wagner, the King and *The Waste Land*' (*Pennsylvania State University Studies*, 1967, pp. 1–87) has almost certainly found more there than Eliot intended or put in, though it is true that Ludwig was drowned (and, as it happens, in the Starnbergersee). One critic has even connected Eliot to Puccini, though his proper place is surely either at the music hall or with the moderns and Stravinsky. Eliot's interest in the music hall is well documented, and there are bawdy songs and ragtime in *The Waste Land* (and I like the idea of Tiresias as master of ceremonies introducing the 'turns'!). His friendship with Stravinsky has been traced by Robert Craft ('Stravinsky and Eliot', *Encounter*, Jan 1978, pp. 46–57), and we know he was deeply moved by a performance of *Le Sacre du Printemps* to the point of hitting with his umbrella neighbours in the audience who were laughing. Whether we see this (as Pinkney does) as responding to the sight of someone 'doing a woman in' and a 'male audience marshalled against its female victim' is another matter. Because it interests me, I am prepared to follow Knust but not Pinkney. Analogy and source-hunting, in other words, can be distracting. Nevertheless, reading T. S. Eliot probably requires us to read four authors (all, incidentally, writers in exile): Ovid, Dante (the *Vita Nuova*, and the *Divina Commedia*), James Joyce (*Ulysses* and possibly *Finnegans Wake*) and Ezra Pound (*The Cantos*), which is the work of a lifetime.

But the pleasures of reading Eliot are also immediate. Even *Finnegans Wake*, Joyce promised us, would come clear if the reader listened to the music. Both *The Waste Land* and *Ash Wednesday* are impressively musical, not as an analogy but in themselves, as we say the words over. The only thing reading Eliot criticism teaches us is that we have to establish as accurately as possible what that haunting music tells us and how it produces the strong feelings that criticism can only begin to explain. Then, and only then, can theory or ideology come in and then, of course, they are not needed. To do this the quester must ask four questions.

Plot and/or story

I. A. Richards maintains that it is a misapplication of energy to try to find a 'narrative' in *The Waste Land*, while Helen Gardner argues that it is a mistake to look for 'development' in *Ash Wednesday*, since the parts were written separately and not even in the order they follow in the completed poem. Eliot's method seems to have been to work in fragments,

which (if he was lucky) cohered in his mind, or, in the case of
Four Quartets, grew from one poem into four. So it is not
really perverse to look at both these poems as if they had an
order or development and, more importantly, a unity. True,
in the case of *The Waste Land* another kind of order may have
been imposed by the editorial hand of Ezra Pound, but the
draft versions suggest he did very little to disturb what the
poem was doing. The appearance of the facsimile edition
may have cast doubts on some earlier treatments but it has
added little. Before the appearance of this edition, it was
possible to hint that Eliot had had a more clear-cut poem
(though Eliot emphatically denied this), but apart from
shifting the emphasis from the social to the personal (and
there had always been readers aware of the personal aspect
of the poem) Mrs Eliot's edition shows that the original
manuscript was even more fragmentary. Pound's revisions
did not give the poem form, but they did reduce the number
of fragments. And looking at the original drafts it is difficult
to believe that the plan and much of the incidental symbolism
were suggested by Weston or that *The Golden Bough* (Frazer's,
nor Virgil's) had much relevance. The Grail legend was not
part of the plan, only part of the organisation. As with
biography, the revelations of the published manuscript have
enriched perceptions of the poem, not muddled them.

When building a house some scaffolding is desirable, and
if readers mistake the scaffolding for the poem that is
unfortunate, but less so than that the poems should lose
readers for want of it. John Peter is probably right when he
suggests that most readers need a story-line to read the poem
before passing to critics such as Leavis or Grover Smith, but
it should be the simplest of threads, not controversial but
basic and pragmatic. Williamson (1953) sees *The Waste Land*
as a poem about the experience that sends a character to a
fortune-teller, the fortune is told and it unfolds, but he then
insists that this story is adumbrated with 'myth' – so much
so that it tends to get lost. For Grover Smith (1956) – who
can be very daunting to an ordinary reader – the poem
summarises the Grail legend: not in the usual order but
retaining all the principal incidents adapted to a modern
setting. Thus all the characters are questers and have to be
connected in terms of the 'information' we obtain through

the allusions. My own view is that if the story/narrative is there to give confidence, it will have to work before the *allusions*, or mainly so. It can only be 'mainly so', since the title clearly refers us to Jessie L. Weston. But, as Brooks and Warren rightly insist (*Understanding Poetry*, 1950), *The Waste Land* is a difficult poem but the allusions (which can be sought out) and the foreign languages (which can be translated) are not the difficulty. We must read the whole poem or, as they express it, gain 'an imaginative apprehension of the poem', and then the reader will have enough respect for it to resist 'being overwhelmed by the commentary'.

The waste land is a kingdom ruled over by a maimed and impotent king, the Fisher King, whose castle stands on the banks of a river. Until the king is healed of his wound, the land is cursed, and he can only be healed when a knight arrives at the castle and asks the meaning of various objects shown to him. Jessie L. Weston saw this as originally a fertility cult, the story of a vegetation god disseminated by soldiers and Syrian merchants and later Christianised into the Grail legends, where the candidate for initiation sought out the Chapel Perilous around which demons howl. Such a candidate must actively seek the truth by asking questions so that he can learn that life and death are related, that the way to life was through death. Much of this is obviously in the poem: Tarot, Syrian merchants, Phlebas, Chapel Perilous; and the Waste Land is clearly a world that has been drained of religious or spiritual meaning. Each reader (like the quester) can remove the curse only if he/she asks questions about what the poem shows us, the meaning of the images. References to the Bible and Dante (Ezekiel, Ecclesiastes and the *Inferno*) add further views of sterile places. Thus any puzzle over lines 69–70, where a character called Stetson is somehow involved with a battle at Mylae, is no puzzle if we see that the Dante quotation (which Eliot tells us is there) applies not only to the crowds going to work in contemporary London but to everyone everywhere: the souls in Hell are gathered from every time and place.

The 'I' of the poem is timid (cf. Prufrock) in a world that is tired, uneasy, apprehensive of the future, yet eager for signs if unwilling to believe in them. This hero has his fortune told in part I, where the dead are buried without hope (unlike the rituals that the poem recalls which promised a new spring or the Resurrection). Part II gives us pictures of life in this waste land – chosen from both the rich and the poor – but in either case sterility prevails and love is absent. Part III is set by the river, which is no longer the highway to social life and marriage ceremonies or even tragic and illicit love affairs; the river is now strewn with debris and witnesses only casual copulation in modern times. Part IV brings about death by drowning, and part V journeys through a landscape where the lack of water induces delirium. By using Sanskrit, the poet extends his references back to the earliest history of the race and its languages. No rain falls, but the resolution – bitter or resigned according to taste – to put one's lands in order is made: the ruins will be shored up, albeit by fragments.

This is in no sense a plot, but it gives some idea of moving forward which, if false (both poems after all are theme and variations rather than symphonic in structure), may help to hold the fragments together, induce confidence, respect and research.

With *Ash Wednesday* the task seems easier, though the nature of the experience is inescapably difficult and possibly exclusive. Difficult (and exclusive) because religious. Where in *The Waste Land* both believer and agnostic can grasp the nature of what is happening, here at least the believer is better informed. Pound, as we have seen, is not to be blamed for having obscured the point of view in *The Waste Land*, because he did not, but the point of view in *Ash Wednesday* provides an obvious consistency. As Grover Smith (1956) suggests, the 'I' – whatever substantiality we grant or deny it – gives the poem on the pages a clear development: 'Its monologuist is a man plunged almost into despair.' For Smith, therefore, the poem reflects the continuing conflict in Eliot between flesh (sensuous memories) and the spirit (striving for union with the Word). Grace is represented by the dream visitor in part IV and, if her identity is never made clear, the imagery focuses our attention on the Blessed Virgin and a lady who honours her in meditation. The lady in this vision can mediate between the two, guiding the 'I' towards the divine: thus the hyacinth girl (fertility, sexual love) has become a Beatrice, and the 'I' seeks to be patient without her until the separation is ended. It is clearly a reluctant exile rather than the willed refusal of St John of the Cross. So part I opens with an ambiguity that runs through the poem and announces the two themes – the hopelessness of a return to God, with, as an extra layer, the problem of an artist's failure to create. Medieval writers (and Dante was working within a tradition) often invoked their love (of whatever kind) as a muse to give them inspiration. Cavalcanti asks his *ballata* to carry the news of his illness and grief to his lady in Tuscany (who may, according to Grover Smith, be his wife, recalling that *Ash Wednesday* was originally dedicated to Vivienne). The impotence is no longer the condition of *The Waste Land* but an inability to achieve either passion or devotion in a new set of values: separation, exile, the hopelessness of turning have ended a way of life and are a kind of death. Part II shows the joy in accepting this death. The three leopards function ambivalently. They are predatory and may signify the enemies of the soul – the world, the flesh and the Devil (and could be connected with Dante's leopard and the dog in *The Waste Land*). But white is the colour not simply of uncleanness but also of mourning and purity. The leopards leave the clean bones waiting for resurrection. Elijah under the juniper tree brings in similar associations of life and death. Unger (1966, p. 51ff.) has found a source in Jakob Grimm's tale 'The Juniper Tree', where a childless couple acquire a boy by supernatural means. But, when the wife dies in childbirth, the man marries again and his second wife, who has a daughter, Marlinchen, hates the boy. She kills him, making puddings of his flesh, which the husband eats. But Marlinchen carries the bones to a juniper tree, where a bird appears singing of the boy's death. After killing the stepmother, the bird once more becomes the boy. We must also remember that, when Elijah was threatened by Jezebel for destroying the prophets of Baal (1 Kings 19), he fled into the wilderness and sat under a juniper tree praying for death. But an angel came and fed him. The bones also recall Ezekiel (ch. 37) and as a consequence of dismemberment remind us that Osiris was torn to pieces by Set. Part III climbs the stairs, a purgatorial experience because it is recalled after part II, and the speaker meets images of himself, darkness and finally, in the May Day vision, of beguilement, though the sin here is venial – as Thomas says in *Murder in the Cathedral*, not worth forgetting.

But this purgatorial vision can recover time, giving the lost years of hope, love and creativity a new meaning. The Lady does not speak because she is withdrawn and the poet in exile. Thus renunciation (part I) is complemented by symbolic death (part II) followed by memories of the past (parts III and IV), lost because the word was missing that might fulfil sensuality or make the vision actual. The Word [Christ] remains, but the right desire is needed and prayer – a word – is necessary. So part VI returns to Cavalcanti's 'perché': 'Because' is now 'Although'. Yet longing naturally breaks in and patience is needed: for the defeat of one attitude no longer means victory for the other. Such a plot, as Grover Smith (1956) concedes, grows out of the allusions to other writers and is not innocent of 'what looks like wilful mystification'. The beginner may prefer Williamson (1953) and his more thematic approach. The title reminds us of a day of humility and the poem suggests the Mass 'at many points'. In the ritual for Ash Wednesday the priest, making the sign of the cross on the forehead, says: 'Remember, man, that thou art dust, and unto dust thou shalt return'. This gives the poem its basic theme and since it reminds us of the exile from Eden (Genesis, 3) 'implies the complementary theme'. Thus we no longer have fear in a handful of dust but rather recognition of the basic promise of that handful of dust. The poem turns between the world (a desert or waste land) and God (a garden). In part I the speaker says that, having lost ambition and energy he gives up the struggle. He hopes he will never again turn to the world, because there things – even religion – are limited. He must begin again, without hope, and he prays for mercy. Part II rejoices in the acceptance of death, and the leopards, if agents of destruction, are beautiful because they cleanse by removing the self so that the speaker no longer laments the frustrations that the self suffers. Part III is in the manner of Dante (but without Dante's confidence?), presenting the speaker with visions of evil, doubt, despair and a tempting recollection of spring and youth. In part IV the Lady becomes the Mother, leading in to part V: the Word. Part VI can then allow the world to return and there is a vision of beauty, but the despair of part I has now been clarified: the intellectual soul (and presumably the poet who deals in images?) cannot follow the negative way.

Such schemes are, palpably, inadequate, but they may get the reader through the poem, inspiring confidence and respect – and then research.

Allusions

Since such 'plots' mainly grow out of the allusions, and since few of us are so firmly rooted in culture (as Eliot saw it) not to need footnotes, that research will start with the allusions. It may be true, as Leavis suggests, that most of the allusions would be known to those who read modern poetry; it may be true, as Matthiessen suggests, that they are no worse than the allusions in Milton, which no one complains about (though my students do complain and, of course, Milton not only had a story-line but his allusions are objective not personal); it may be true, as Bush says, that we are to grasp the mood rather than work out the sources (but how do we recognise the mood if we do not know the sources?); it may be true, as Brooks says, that they can be pointed to and the foreign languages translated for us, but the situation is never as simple as that. It is true that Eliot achieved impersonality (and invisibility) by using other people's literary versions of his own feelings: thus the poems are a series of objective correlatives and thus, too, in a major sense, the allusions *are* the poems. And, as Grover Smith (1983) notes, they have a 'peculiar prominence' because Eliot paraded them and in a particularly prankish way, so that *The Waste Land*, at least on one level, can be seen as a 'burlesque myth'. Since they are important but personal and since their use is often arbitrary or whimsical, the apparently simple pointing-out and/or translation can be surprisingly difficult. Consider the opening of part I, which I had always considered to be an obvious echo of Chaucer and the Prologue to *The Canterbury Tales*, where a group of characters representative of society gather together, liberated by spring, to go on a pilgrimage. Thus Eliot establishes the Prologue-like nature of part I, its contrasts, and introduces a group of characters who will wander through the landscape of the poem telling their stories. But neither Brooks (1947) nor Williamson (1953) nor Grover Smith (1983) bothers to mention Chaucer, and, while Southam (1969) admits that critics generally contrast this opening with Chaucer (though not as frequently as I thought), he offers Rupert Brooke's poem 'The Old Vicarage, Grantchester' with its recollection of childhood and an English spring contrasted with present-day life in Berlin. Brooke's poem also includes the lilacs. But I had always understood (from the late Norman Holmes Pearson) that the lilacs in line 2 should recall the funeral of President Lincoln and the Whitman poem 'When Lilacs Last in the Dooryard Bloom'd'.

The Wagner references in part I (which Eliot gives us in his notes) show how allusion often works to involve larger works: the epic in a nutshell. To a certain extent we are obliged to respond to the garden scene which these phrases enclose in terms of the opera *Tristan and Isolde* (and indeed in one way Eliot involves the whole of *The Ring* and *Parsifal* in his poem!). The title drives us to myth, but the overall (or under-all) pattern of myth presents difficulties, too. Does the pattern order the poem, or does the critic find order in the poem by imposing a pattern? For a minor example of the dangers one has only to consider the casual way in which Eliot uses the Tarot pack – surely as little more than a list of *dramatis personae* in his prologue? Charles Williams shows, in his novel *The Greater Trumps* (1932), how the Tarot pack could be used.

Grover Smith's complex note on the dog ('God' backwards according to some critics) ignores what I was taught – namely, that when Isis went looking for the pieces of Osiris she took her dogs, who dug up the pieces. Osiris is, of course, both the vegetation god who dies and is reborn, the Nile which rises and falls, and God of the Dead (his counsellor, incidentally, was Hermes Trismegistus, whose book is said to have provided the Major Arcana for the Tarot pack). When Osiris was murdered by Set, the coffer in which his body was enclosed floated to the coast of Phoenicia, whence it was recovered. Isis hid it but Set rediscovered it and cut it up into fourteen pieces, scattered far and wide, which Isis found (except the phallus, which had been eaten by a Nile crab, a creature forever cursed) and she remade the body (establishing the practice of embalming) and, by magic, became the mother of Horus.

Clearly the wolf in Webster is a foe and the dog is a friend; dogs in general symbolise faithfulness and, as sheepdogs, priests of the church. The dog also accompanies the dead on their crossing and is associated with resurrection. In fact, both dog and wolf figure on the Moon card in the Tarot pack – though in some packs the picture shows two dogs! Is all this the wild-goose chase lamented by Eliot – with tongue in cheek?

Consider the character of Phlebas, whose name could mean, 'You are weeping'. But, according to Grover Smith, we should also note that the name could derive from the Greek *phléps*, *phlébos* – 'vein', which has, as its secondary meaning, the sense 'phallus'. Hence we should recall Osiris of the triple phallus (*The Golden Bough*) and the Man with Three Staves.

When Pound omitted things, he knew (and we can too) what he had omitted, but with Eliot meaning seems to tumble around in his imagination and perhaps that must happen to us, too. The logic of the imagination – of *his* imagination – is what matters and we can only use common sense. If an allusion helps, it works. Grover Smith reminds us that between the allusions we recognise or those claimed in the notes and other sources the correlation is so incomplete that a sense of playfulness runs through everything. We can sense this, perhaps in lines 199–201, where Mrs Porter and her daughter wash their feet in soda water. Getting the right soda water (not the drink, that is) is only the beginning. As prostitutes they will naturally be footsore, and the reference neatly recalls Maundy Thursday, which leads to Good Friday in the subsequent *Parsifal* quotation (but Verlaine not Wagner!). Mrs Porter was, we are told, a legendary brothel-keeper in Cairo, and Southam thinks that Eliot might have heard a polite version of the song. Grover Smith notes that there are many versions as sung by soldiers, and it is not her feet that Mrs Porter washes. But the inventor of King Bolo probably knew exactly what he was doing. In 1915 Wyndham Lewis wrote to Pound that Eliot had sent him 'Bullshit' and the 'Ballad for Big Louise', which he longed to print in *Blast*, but he was sticking to his determination not to have words 'ending in -Uck, -Unt and -Ugger'. And Eliot still shows this side of his nature in 1949 when the uses in *The Cocktail Party* the song about One-Eyed Reilly (and his daughter) – a song of which, I suspect, there are no polite versions. The note to *The Waste Land* on the hermit thrush (*Turdus . . .*) is another example of fun and scholarship parodied. So in the end each reader's ideas may prove satisfactory but none can be final.

With *Ash Wednesday* the basic difficulty is Dante. But Hugh Kenner in *The Pound Era* (1972) reminds us that some things were current which no longer exist, and one of these was a public for inexpensive bilingual editions of Dante. By looking at the publication history of editions of the *Divina Commedia* starting in 1899, he shows that there was a taste for what is now 'dug for in research collections'. Thus in 1909–10 Pound gave a series of lectures at the Polytechnic in Regent Street on Dante, Daniel and the Troubadours, and, when, in 1923, the Malatesta Cantos were written, Pound nowhere felt the need to tell the reader who Sigismundo was – he assumed people would know. Thus, by 1934, R. P. Blackmur thought the subject-matter recondite, and yet, as Kenner observes, all that half-century numbers attending university had been growing. Poets of Pound's generation were searching for the language of the tribe (hence Eliot's work on Sanskrit) and it is noteworthy that Otto Jespersen's pioneer study *Language: Its Nature, Development and Origins* was published in 1922. This said, the real problem in *Ash Wednesday* is not the allusions so much as the nature of the experience described in the poem. If *The Waste Land* is an act of love in our lives, *Ash Wednesday* is an act of faith: and faith resists criticism.

Unity

The main purpose of either finding a 'story' or understanding the allusions is to inspire confidence in the reader that the poem has meaning, has some sense of unity, though we must be careful to find the unity in the poem and not merely in the interpretation. Whether unity is necessary or desirable and what we mean by 'unity' are questions to tease a seminar but perhaps of less importance elsewhere. Clearly the matter of unity (or lack of it) is something that has bothered many readers and critics, though the puzzlement is more understandable among early readers of Eliot's poetry, since they had been brought up in the Victorian narrative tradition. Today's film-goers should have little difficulty with the montage. Eliot's method was in a way cinematic: he glued together bits of poetry and pretended that he was only a camera (the editorship theory fashionable at the time), but obviously words have to be written by someone. So we invent a 'story' to confer unity on a poem, such as *The Waste Land*, that seems to lack it. Some critics have made a virtue out of fragments by pointing out that one theme of the poem is the fragmented nature of contemporary society, so that the only way to present it dramatically would be in fragments. But it is surely the business of an artist to make a whole of fragments? The glue was mainly personal and the emotions of the poem were filtered through literary works that echoed personal feeling but in an impersonal (because second-hand) way. The 'story' often seems to bend the poem in a way that is not entirely satisfactory. Grover Smith, for example, sees part II as looking at sex without love in marriage, and part III as sex without love outside marriage. This makes the man with Belladonna specifically her husband, not her lover, so the noise in line 118 cannot be the fear of a detective looking for evidence of adultery (as I was taught) and some of the force of a 'closed car' seems to be lost. However, on the evidence of the manuscript, the closed car only appears because Eliot needed the taxi for part III.

In the *Paris Review* interview (1959) Eliot denied that Pound had made the poem structureless, confessing that it was 'just as structureless, only in a more futile way, in the longer version'. My own feeling is that the problem does not exist and that one way of showing that it does not is to listen to the poem as if it were a play for voices. They are, after all, curiously disembodied voices, hinting at the problem that would face Eliot when he turned to drama. Ironically, Eliot noted the difficulty when writing about Browning in 'The Three Voices of Poetry' (1953): if few of us can forget Fra Lippo Lippi or Andrea del Sarto or the bishop who ordered his tomb, who can remember a personage from a Browning play? The first play produced specially for radio was broadcast in 1924, and, if we compare *The Waste Land* with *Under Milk Wood*, we can see that both are plays with voices that build up a picture of a place. The London of *The Waste Land* is a place like Llaregub (or Joyce's Dublin): so in the prologue one end of London Bridge is where pilgrims set off for Canterbury, and over the bridge on the right is Magnus Martyr (with its Ionian splendour of white and gold) and straight ahead the Monument to the Great Fire that burned the bridge down.

Eliot's note on Tiresias (added later) is an attempt to give the poem a 'point of view', and so Grover Smith (1983) – who finds two kinds of unity in the poem (psychological and cultural) – insists that the unity is in Tiresias, which is appropriate because it was Tiresias who 'saw' the cause of the curse laid on Thebes (another waste land). The Tiresias note (he suggests) *explains* the nature of the structure: Tiresias contemplates ('and being the poet, stylistically renders') the material. Thus Gerontion – Grover Smith points out (1956) – which Eliot had wanted to use as a prelude to the whole poem – becomes Tiresias and combines 'spiritual acuteness and emotional impotence'. The modern figure is replaced by a mythological one to unify the parts of *The Waste Land*. He does so in a most complex way, however. Tiresias is, for example, a hermaphrodite which Grover Smith claims mirrors the sin of Arnaut in *Purgatorio XXVI*. This is not to be taken, we are warned, as an account of Eliot's personal behaviour but as a way of writing about psychology and sex in a bold manner fashionable in 1921. Tiresias brings psychological ideas into focus and combines 'a primitive social psychology' with an advanced modern individual psychology. The Provencal poet Arnaut is, of course, the original *miglior fabbro* and Dante meets him in Canto 26 among the Penitents of Natural and Unnatural Lust. There are two troops of penitents and the one in which Arnaut is to be found say: 'Nostro peccato fu ermafrodito'. Thus Arnaut is not to be confused with unnatural lust (sodomy); his sin is innocent of offence against the Natural Law but he has contravened the Human Law by behaving in a brutish (but heterosexual) manner ('seguendo come bestie l'appetito'). Thus the image of their sin is Pasiphaë who, hidden in the effigy of a cow built for her by Daedalus, satisfied her craving and mated with a bull – giving birth to the Minotaur.

Grover Smith (1983) produces a formidable list of sources (Fitzgerald, Tennyson, Matthew Arnold, Dryden, Milton, James Joyce, Aldous Huxley, *The Golden Bough*, the *Brihadaranyaka- Upanishad* and Edward Carpenter) but Eliot's note points to Ovid. Here Tiresias, for interfering with the copulation of serpents, is changed into a woman. After seven years he repeats the offence and becomes a man again. He is thus, unfortunately, in a position to arbitrate in a dispute between Jupiter and Juno on the relative pleasures of sex as between man and woman. When he judges in favour of Jupiter, Juno strikes him blind but Jupiter, to mitigate the punishment, gives him the gift of prophecy. Another source must be Apollinaire's play *Les Mamelles de Tirésias* (1918) where the prophet is both Tirésias and Thérèse and so has the 'female breasts' which he certainly has not in Ovid.

As a character, Grover Smith concedes, Tiresias is more shadowy than Gerontion, who clearly speaks the poem of that name; nevertheless *The Waste Land* is *his* reverie (it is he who speaks the opening lines and he is in the poem from the very beginning): a stream-of-consciousness technique reminiscent of Joyce. But it strikes one again – like the famous review of *Ulysses* – that Eliot creates the note to justify what he had done. We have a mythological character to unify diversity and both sexes reminding us that some of the voices are female. This may remove the difficulty of the episode with Mr Eugenides (line 208) which Eliot was surprised to find being interpreted as a homosexual encounter. But surely his note is whimsical, too? Nineteen lines of Latin – 'of great anthropological interest'! Tiresias is, indeed, the only explicit identification of a speaker in the poem but when Williamson (1953), for example, describes the episode as an interruption that seems to be just the right word. Williamson begins his discussion – as we have seen – in terms of the poem 'Dans le Restaurant': Dante and the New Life rather than Ovid. In 'Dans le Restaurant', a dirty old waiter recalls his first sexual experience, which took place when he was seven and was interrupted by a large dog (no friend to man here). The diner rebukes him and gives him ten sous for a bath, but clearly feels guilty, because he, too, has had a similar experience. All this echoes Dante's *Vita Nuova*, which, Williamson feels, becomes relevant in *The Waste Land* to Fisher King myth and modern reality. In Jessie Weston, sex has both universal and religious significance connected with the state of the land (the waste land, as she calls it), so we are to see the Fisher King as the prototype of all the characters who speak in the poem, even in the Tiresias 'interruption'. It is the myth of the Fisher King which unifies the poem. Weston, of course, connects Lance and Grail with sexual symbolism in the four suits of the Tarot and sees a double scheme in the story: initiation into the Lower Mysteries (those of sexual generation) and the Higher Mystery (man made one with God). So, for Williamson, every character is 'mythically' connected. Clearly from both examples the unity stems from a story interpreting the allusions, but, as we have seen, Tiresias and the symbolism seem to have been part of the organisation of the poem after it had been written – and edited.

Perhaps it is time to see just how difficult the poem is? Let us consider part I. Because the epigraph is in Latin (and Petronius's Latin is macaronic, not of the best and jazzed up with Greek), most of us will have to look it up. The Sybil had asked Apollo for as many years as she held grains of sand in her hand; she forgot to ask for eternal youth as well! On her better days the Sybil wrote down her messages on leaves which were laid outside the cave door – where the wind could disturb them. In any case, the messages were couched in riddles which left the inquirer in doubt (Tiresias, too, will not answer Oedipus, but gives him a puzzle about an oar that has been mistaken for a winnowing fan). Readers of Hopkins's poem 'Spelt from Sybil's Leaves' will already be familiar with this; they will also remember that the Sybil figures in the *Dies Irae*, that terrible celebration of the Day of Judgement that used to be said or sung at every Requiem Mass. This mediator between this world and the gods is no longer consulted by the great but is tormented by curious boys. So both theme (life, death, religion, prophecy, greatness in the past and a shrunken present) and method – fragments in riddles – have been announced as we turn the page to read 'The Burial of the Dead'. The title here recalls the Book of Common Prayer and the comfortable words of St Paul that 'the dead shall be raised incorruptible, and we shall all be changed', immediately denied as Chaucer is denied. This April brings no 'vertu', nor do people long to go on pilgrimages. Instead we have a tour of fashionable Europe. The lilacs may recall Whitman and the funeral of President Lincoln or simply an English spring unwelcome because it awakens us to memory and desire, to recollections of a full life. A particular memory of sunshine and a shower of rain introduces a childhood memory – not, I suspect, as Grover Smith (1983) suggests, of a Lithuanian lady. The line in German surely recalls the date – some time just after 1919, when aristocratic Russians were refugees, while the archduke summons up the image of the collapsed Austro-Hungarian Empire: a post-war world in which nothing exists, and the only quest is to go south after the sun in winter. The memory of the sleigh ride is fearful but also exhilarating.

From this opening the poet (for it is surely not Tiresias?) asks, what are the roots that bind us to a place and nourish us? 'Son of man' is first a reference to Ezekiel but more obviously to Christ, and the first nourishing factor is religion. Grover Smith finds the red rock obscure, but this may be because he wishes it to fit in with the Grail. More simply, the rock is Peter and the Church, and red is the colour of saints and martyrs who committed themselves to the Church even unto death and so nourish it. To commit oneself to religion would bring the consolations of religion in this harsh world ('the shadow of this red rock') but with that come consequences: 'fear in a handful of dust'. For, in accepting the comforts of religion, one accepts also the concept of life in this vale of tears as only a preparation for the true life in Heaven – or, if we are not careful, Hell. We cannot be sure. So the poet turns to romantic love and the episode in the hyacinth garden. We have probably not read *The Golden Bough* (it is, after all, twelve volumes long) but we know the story of Hyacinthus, a young man beloved of Apollo, Boreas and Zephyrus. One day when Apollo and Hyacinthus were throwing the discus, Boreas and Zephyrus, being winds, jealously blew the discus thrown by Apollo so that it struck Hyacinthus on the head and killed him. As the blood spurted out, the flower grew which bears his name. So wind, blood, slain god and resurrection; and, moreover, the flower looks like a male sexual symbol. The sexuality of this passage if probed is suspicious, but need not lead us astray; again failure to commit oneself to love means an opportunity missed. The references to *Tristan and Isolde* (now given us by Eliot) reinforce this theme. Even if we do not exactly know the details of this tangle of magic potion, love, betrayal and death (with a wind that augurs well but fails in the last act), we recognise a couple who were capable of dying for love – recaptured later by Dido or Cleopatra. The third transcendental force in the lives of men – magic – has shrunk too; the Sybil (already past her best) is now Madame Sosostris, a wise woman with a bad cold, harried by the police and serving the likes of 'dear Mrs Equitone'. The instruments of power – the Tarot – are now reduced to mere fortune-telling. It is perfectly appropriate, therefore, for Eliot to use them 'quite arbitrarily' as a list of characters who will occupy the poem, though most readers will identify the absence of the Hanged Man as being some sort of reference to the Crucifixion.

These characters from every time and place are in Hell, but the unreal city at least begins with crowds flowing over London Bridge to start work – a mechanical life removed from the seasons which expresses itself in a flurry of references. Grover Smith warns us at this point that there is danger 'lest multiplied allusions, adventitious or not, should defeat meaning' (1983, p. 79)! Suffice it, then, that the line from Baudelaire reminds us that this is only an introduction to the poem. Pound, I think, is right when he says that *The Waste Land* is an emotional unit and its total effect demands no great knowledge of the sources, though Pound's habit of mind was such as to relish this kind of poetry, as his own *Cantos* monumentally show.

As far as *Ash Wednesday* is concerned, because of its pervasive (if elusive) 'I' there are no problems of unity. Helen Gardner's objection that the parts were written separately and in another order does not alter our sense of unity and development. The difficulties here remain with the meaning, which, since it seems to grow out of the allusions, throws a heavy burden on the reader. Moreover, where in *The Waste Land* feeling purged of self because out of literature is appropriate, even a non-religious reader must baulk at mystical experience that comes second-hand.

Theme

The theme of both poems, a theme that runs through all Eliot's poetry and plays and on which variations are played, is death – a word, of course, which covers a multitude of paradoxes. This theme is announced on the title page of *The Waste Land* by the Sybil. Cleanth Brooks's analysis of the poem (1939) is in terms drawn from the essay on Baudelaire, where the loss of the knowledge of Good and Evil prevents us from being alive. The central paradox of the poem (he suggests) is that life without meaning is really a kind of death, while sacrifice, even unto death, may be life-giving. Thus in part I death is attractive as even more final than death-in-life (and Eliot must, one supposes, have had Coleridge at the back of his mind), while 'A Game of Chess' illustrates how life without meaning is a kind of death, though Eliot makes constant reference to the dying-God theme in the poem. In 'The Fire Sermon' the fire is lust but sterile, and Eliot reminds us that both Buddha and St Augustine (East and West) use the image of fire. Yet fire purges too, and when Arnaut Daniel has finished his speech we are told, '*Poi s'ascose nel foco che gli affina*' ('Then he hid him in the fire which refines them'). From fire the poet turns to water (parts IV and V), and again it is the water that drowns and the water that baptises. Eliot is seen, therefore, as renewing Christian clichés (i.e. positively Christian). But it is no detriment to the poem to recognise that this is the insight of hindsight.

The Baudelaire essay is dated 1930. Eliot was reviewing a translation of Baudelaire's *Journaux intimes* and claiming for the author a more important role than that of the writer of *Les Fleurs du mal*; to see him as a 'fragmentary Dante' (the complement to the *Journaux intimes*, we are told, is the *Vita Nuova* and the *Divina Commedia*), an essentially Christian poet. Baudelaire discovers Christianity for himself, not so much to practise it as to assert its '*necessity*' ('Genuine blasphemy . . . is the product of partial belief'). So Baudelaire is a modern poet concerned not with black masses and romantic demons but 'with the real problem of good and evil'. The possibility of damnation is a great relief from the ennui of modern life because it gives significance to living: the recognition of sin is a New Life, for a notion of sin implies a sense of the good. The relationship between man and woman is different from the animals because of this knowledge. So because we are human we must do either good or evil, and in doing either good or evil we show ourselves to be human. From this it follows that it is better to do evil than nothing, because it shows we exist.

Eliot's view of Baudelaire's view of women is interesting also. Baudelaire's vision of beatitude is restricted, so there is a gap between human and divine love. Where his idea of human love is positive, divine love is vague and uncertain: 'hence his insistence upon the evil of love, hence his constant vituperation of the female'. There is no need, Eliot remarks, to seek psychopathological causes for this (they would be irrelevant): his attitude towards women is consistent with the point of view which he had reached. Was Eliot, I wonder, recalling his own view of women in *The Waste Land*, to be translated, by idealisation, into the Lady of *Ash Wednesday*, an idealisation many find as disturbing as the presentation of women in *The Waste Land*? Eliot's handling of women in *The Waste Land* was perhaps nothing more than choosing them as examples of love and fertility (and hence handing down values from one time to another) which had been lost. His disgust was possibly sharpened by his personal predicament, though all the evidence points to a large and helpful involvement of Vivienne in writing the poem.

In making the poem Christian (which *potentially* it is), we should not overlook Grover Smith's comment (1983) on the final note to line 433, which originally read, 'The Peace which Passeth All Understanding is a feeble translation of the content of this word.' This, after 1925, became simply the present note: '. . . is our equivalent of the word'. Not, as Smith remarks, a whisper of hope but heavily ironic and confirming, surely, all the implications of line 30: 'I will show you fear in a handful of dust'.

The connection between morals and literature is more

obvious in *Ash Wednesday*, though we should remember Eliot's insistence that poetry is not a substitute for philosophy or religion. It has a function of its own which is emotional not intellectual. Yet we must, surely, know *how* we feel? Death is welcomed but it is a complex kind of death. If story and unity seem easier in *Ash Wednesday*, the allusions are not, and, since they inform the poem with its meaning (a difficult meaning too), reading the poem is not easy. The New Life required a New Style. In 'Salutation' (part II) – the first poem in order of composition – Eliot originally provided an epigraph: '*e voi significando*'. This takes us back to Dante's meeting with Bongiunta Lucca (*Purgatorio*, XXIV), who hails Dante as the poet of '*il dolce stil nuovo*': this sweet new style. Other poets of the new style include Dante's friend Cavalcanti, but Dante is credited with the resolution of the antinomy implicit in courtly love: sexual love at its most exalted is one manifestation of the Divine Love which moves the universe and which takes in and fulfils all lesser loves (as in the *Vita Nuova*). **According to Eliot, Dante's allegorical method makes for** simplicity and intelligibility – for the competent poet, 'clear visual images'; and Matthiessen suggests that the best audience for this poem would be one who can neither read nor write: the poem makes an impression through the beauty of its sound and then with a lucidity that is poetic not intellectual. But we are struck, I suspect, by the argument of the poem, illustrated by images that are clear because visual but obscure to any other sense. Eliot, at any rate, first used the 'new style' in 'Salutation'.

Ash Wednesday, a poem written in exile and full of despair and weariness, and in which worship of the Lady is the only redeeming force, opens with an invocation of Cavalcanti; a line from Shakespeare reinforces (and expands) this. The poet is sorting things out (hence the repetitive language) and exploring the failure of the individual and the labours of reason, will and art. By part II, grace is present. The vision here is not so much death of the body as death of the self assisted by the Lady and, as a corollary, the Church and the communion of saints. Part III shows that both the visions of desert and lady are over: they may have helped but the struggle is now resumed. The 'I' has to turn and turn as he mounts the stair facing views on each landing: himself, darkness and finally the distractions through the window. Part IV returns to the dream, but it is now Dante's 'higher dream'. Since life is exile, death is enviable, but death in the widening circumstances of part V: a world circling about the Word; the Incarnation and the Passion – both words uniting flesh and spirit in a most intimate way. This leads us into the final part, which recalls part I. Conflict, refreshing sights but also aspiration, and the wings are no longer aged but unbroken. The poet faces the sea, which, as 'Marina' makes clear, is no longer '*Oed' und leer*'.

But the difficult nature, the transitional feel of the poem is unmistakable. Even for a reader trained in religion and/or Dante, the nature of the experience remains somehow distant. W. H. Pritchard (1980) is speaking for many when he describes it as 'poetic behaviour one never feels comfortable in responding to'. Bergonzi (1972) reports that Eliot in Cambridge spent an evening talking with an Italian Marxist and afterwards noted how certain his belief was. His own, he said, was held with a scepticism 'which I never even hope to be quite rid of' (p. 113). Eliot may have recognised the joy of faith intellectually, but it appears only fitfully in the poetry and never in the prose. In *After Strange Gods* Eliot warned that people writing religious verse usually wrote 'what they want to feel, rather than as they do feel', but here Eliot is honest enough to acknowledge that, for him, the struggle with unbelief is not a particularly joyous experience. It is, after all, Ash Wednesday. Like us, he probably wishes the struggle were more joyous, but he will not fake it. We tend, I suspect, to hurry on to *Four Quartets*, where the allusions do not matter but which we can only have because of *Ash Wednesday*. In *Four Quartets* the poet speaks directly to us and vibrantly – if not with joy, at least with a hard-won serenity. Yet all these poems demonstrate that talent which Kenner has described as 'the art of creating with an air of utter precision the feel of concepts one cannot localize'.

Bibliography

This bibliography does not include works published by Eliot; some books and articles are mentioned in passing in the text and identified there; and criticism collected in *T. S. Eliot: The Critical Heritage* (all such items are identified in the text by an asterisk). Other sources may be identified below from name of author and date of publication.

The first two sections of the Bibliography correspond to the two sections of Part One ('Survey'), on *The Waste Land* and *Ash Wednesday*, respectively. Critical studies cited in both sections will be found below under *The Waste Land*. Further background and research material is listed in the third section of the Bibliography ('Other material'), including a few works mentioned but not discussed in Part One. Part Two of the book ('Appraisal') cites sources already cited in Part One, and references may be traced in the first two sections of the Bibliography. All critics discussed may also be traced through the Index.

The Waste Land

Ackroyd, Peter, *T. S. Eliot* (London, 1984).

Brooks, Cleanth, *Modern Poetry and the Tradition* (Chapel Hill, NC, 1939).

Brooks, Van Wyck, *The Confident Years 1885–1915* (London, 1952).

Bush, Ronald, *T. S. Eliot: A Study in Character and Style* (Oxford, 1984).

Cox, C. B., 'T. S. Eliot at the Cross Roads', *Critical Quarterly*, 12 (1970) 307–30.

Craig, David, 'The Defeatism of *The Waste Land*', *Critical Quarterly*, Autumn 1960, pp. 241–52.

Drew, Elizabeth, *T. S. Eliot: The Design of his Poetry* (London, 1949).

Eastman, Max, *The Literary Mind: Its Place in an Age of Science* (New York, 1931).
Empson, William, review of *The Waste Land, Essays in Criticism*, 22 (1972), pp. 417–429.
Foster, G. W., 'The Archetypal Imagery of T. S. Eliot', *PMLA*, 60 (1945) 567–85.
Gordon, Lyndall, *Eliot's Early Years* (Oxford and New York, 1977).
Grant, Michael (ed.), *T. S. Eliot: The Critical Heritage*, 2 vols (London, 1982).
Gross, Harvey, *The Contrived Corridor: History and Fatality in Modern Literature* (Ann Arbor, Mich., 1971).
Hough, Graham, *Reflections on a Literary Revolution* (London, 1960).
Kenner, Hugh, *The Invisible Poet: T. S. Eliot* (New York, 1959, London, 1960).
Kojecký, Roger, *T. S. Eliot's Social Criticism* (London, 1971).
Leavis, F. R., *New Bearings in English Poetry: A Study of the Contemporary Situation* (London, 1932).
Matthews, T. S., *Great Tom: Notes Towards the Definition of T. S. Eliot* (London, 1934).
Matthiessen, F. O., *The Achievement of T. S. Eliot: An Essay on the Nature of Poetry* (London, 1935).
Miller, J. E., *T. S. Eliot's Personal Waste Land: Exorcism of the Demons* (State College, Pa, 1977).
Moorman, Charles, *Arthurian Triptych* (Berkeley, Calif., 1960).
Peter, John, 'A New Interpretation of *The Waste Land*', *Essays in Criticism*, 1952, pp. 242–66; reprinted with a Postscript, 1969, pp. 140–74.
Pinkney, Tony, *Women in the Poetry of T. S. Eliot: A Psychoanalytic Approach* (London, 1984).
Richards, I A., *Principles of Literary Criticism* (New York, 1924, 1926).
Sampley, Arthur, 'The Woman Who Wasn't There: Lacuna in T. S. Eliot', *South Atlantic Quarterly*, Autumn 1968, pp. 603–10.
Schneider, Elizabeth, *T. S. Eliot: The Pattern in the Carpet* (Berkeley, Calif., 1975).
Shapiro, Karl, *In Defense of Ignorance* (New York, 1960).
Smith, Grover, *T. S. Eliot's Poetry and Plays: A Study in Sources and Meaning* (Chicago, 1956).
Smith, Grover, *The Waste Land* (London, 1983).
Stead, C. K., *The New Poetic: Yeats to Eliot* (London, 1964).
Steiner, George, *Language and Silence* (London, 1967).

Strachey, John, *The Coming Struggle for Power* (London, 1932, 1934).
Sultan, Stanley, *'Ulysses', 'The Waste Land', and Modernism* (Port Washington, NY, 1977).
Trosman, Harry, 'T. S. Eliot and *The Waste Land*: Psychopathological Antecedents and Transformations', *Archives of General Psychiatry*, May 1974.
Watson, George, 'Quest for a Frenchman', *Sewanee Review*, 1976, pp. 465–75.
Wilson, Edmund, *Axel's Castle: A Study in the Imaginative Literature of 1870–1930* (New York, 1931).
Williamson, George, *A Reader's Guide to T. S. Eliot* (New York 1953, London 1955).

Ash Wednesday

Boardman, G. R., '*Ash Wednesday*: Eliot's Lenten Mass Sequence', *Renascence*, Fall 1962, pp. 28–36.
Clowder, Felix, 'The Bestiary of T. S. Eliot', *Prairie Schooner*, Spring 1960, pp. 30–7.
Dolan, P. J., '*Ash Wednesday*: A Catechumenical Poem', *Renascence*, Summer 1967, pp. 198–207.
Frye, Northrop, *T. S. Eliot: An Introduction* (Chicago, 1963).
Gardner, Helen, *The Art of T. S. Eliot* (London, 1949).
Jones, E. E. Duncan, '*Ash Wednesday*' in *T. S. Eliot*, ed. B. Rajan (London, 1947) pp. 37–56.
Praz, Mario, 'T. S. Eliot and Dante', *Southern Review*, Winter 1937, pp. 525–48.
Pritchard, W. H., *Lives of the Modern Poets* (London, 1980).
Savage, D. S., *The Personal Principle* (London, 1944).
Spender, Stephen, *Eliot* (Glasgow, 1975).
Unger, Leonard, *T. S. Eliot: Moments and Patterns* (Minneapolis, 1966).
Wooten, Carl, 'The Mass: *Ash Wednesday*'s Objective Correlative', *Arizona Quarterly*, Spring 1961, pp. 31–42.

Other material

Bibliographies

Gallup, Donald, *T. S. Eliot: A Bibliography* (London, 1969).
Martin, Mildred, *A Half Century of Eliot Criticism* (London, 1972).

Chronology

Behr, Caroline, *T. S. Eliot: A Chronology of his Life and Works* (London, 1983).

Memoirs and biography

Chiari, Joseph, *T. S. Eliot: A Memoir* (London, 1982).
Howarth, Herbert, *Notes on Some Figures behind T. S. Eliot* (London, 1965).
Levy, W. T., and Scherle, Victor, *Affectionately, T. S. Eliot. The Story of a Friendship, 1947–65* (London, 1968).
Sencourt, Robert, *T. S. Eliot: A Memoir* (London, 1974).

Critical studies

Braybrooke, Neville (ed.), *T. S. Eliot: A Symposium* (London, 1958).
Bergonzi, Bernard, *T. S. Eliot* (London, 1972).
Canary, R. H., *T. S. Eliot: The Poet and his Critics* (Chicago, 1982).
Cox, C. B., and Hinchliffe, A. P. (eds), *The Waste Land* (London, 1968).
Eliot, Valerie (ed.), *The Waste Land: A Facsimile and Transcript of the Original Drafts* (London, 1971).
Gray, Piers, *Eliot's Intellectual and Poetic Development, 1909–1922* (Brighton, 1982).
Knoll, R. E. (ed.), *Storm over 'The Waste Land'* (Chicago, 1964).
Martin, Jay (ed.), *A Collection of Critical Essays on 'The Waste Land'* (Englewood Cliffs, NJ, 1968).
Rajan, B., *T. S. Eliot: A Study of his Writings by Several Hands* (London, 1947).
Rosenthal, M. L., '*The Waste Land* as an Open Structure', *Mosaic*, 6 (1972) 181–9.

Southam, B. C., *A Guide to the Selected Poems of T. S. Eliot* (London, 1969).

Southam, B. C. (ed.), *'Prufrock', 'Gerontion', 'Ash Wednesday' and Other Shorter Poems* (London, 1978).

Sullivan, Sheila (ed.), *Critics on T. S. Eliot* (London, 1973).

Tate, Allen (ed.), *T. S. Eliot: The Man and his Work* (London, 1967).

Further reading

Buttle, Myra, *The Sweeniad* (London, 1958).

Hastings, Michael, *Tom and Viv*, with an introduction by Michael Hastings (Harmondsworth, Middx, 1985).

Kenner, Hugh, *The Pound Era* (London, 1972).

Reid, B. L., *The Man from New York: John Quinn and his Friends* (New York, 1968).

Russell, Bertrand, *The Autobiography of Bertrand Russell*, ii (London, 1968).

Weston, J. L., *From Ritual to Romance* (Cambridge, 1920).

Williams, Charles, *The Figure of Beatrice* (London, 1943).

86

Index